"THE OTHER CHILD" - ABANDONED

Life in America
Sequel to **The Auschwitz Kommandant**

By

Barbara U. Cherish

"The Other Child" - Abandoned

Copyright © 2013 by Barbara U. Cherish

All Rights Reserved

Edited by Jann J. James - professor of English
And published Author holding a BA in Creative Writing
Also a Masters in English Literature

Some of the names have been changed.

First Edition
Published by Chapters To Go
A Division of Our Hutch LLC
http://chapterstogo.com/

Non Fiction

ISBN-13: 978-1497569980
ISBN-10: 1497569982

Dedicated with Love

To my son Chris

And

Forever in loving memory to

my daughter Whendy

and nephew Kye

and my adopted family
who gave me the opportunity for life in America

"Flowers unfold slowly and gently
bit by bit in the sunshine,
and a soul too, must never be pushed or driven,
but unfolds in its own perfect timing
to reveal its true wonder and beauty."

...The Findhorn Community
Harper Colophon Books, 1975

TABLE OF CONTENTS

Introduction

"Your astrological chart shows a "Cardinal T-Square" which represents a strong degree of difficulty throughout your life. There was something about the timing of your birth that was very difficult for your father. It's not that you weren't wanted, but there was a lot of pressure on him and uncertainty about the coming of this child. It shows he really had bad moments – wondering where things were going and what was going to happen. He felt the timing of your birth at that moment couldn't have been worse and there was a lot of concern about this child coming into this world."

> o   *Donna Eubank Hennen, Astrologer - July 1999.*

My father was Arthur Liebehenschel, once a member of Hitler's SS. I am his youngest daughter, born in Germany during the waning years of WW II - one of *"the other children"* as he called us who were from his first marriage.

The story that follows tells how I had to cast off my identity as one of those *other children* after I was adopted, finding myself living a life of secrecy.

After several revised drafts, four different working titles and almost a decade later I completed my book *The Auschwitz Kommandant - A Daughter's Search for the father she never knew*. I certainly never imagined that my journey into the past would render such a profound psychological impact. Sometimes I found it difficult to distinguish whether I belonged in the past or the present. The memoir is about my family, but most of all it was my desperate need to find out who my father really was because I knew very little - only that he had been a Nazi-SS officer, sentenced to death as a war criminal.

Too young to remember - my research revealed the character of the man who was my father. With an eager personal interest in history I also learned how and why he became involved as Kommandant of the infamous Auschwitz concentration camp. It brought to light how my family, who had lived relatively well during the midst of WW II - was suddenly confronted with the stark reality of mere survival after the war.

As thousands of other displaced families during that time, desperation and poverty overcame us.

My own recollections were of the short time I lived with my two sisters and my mother, who eventually ended up in a mental institution - followed by a childhood in foster homes and finally adoption. That first book and story ended with my arrival in America in December 1956, when I was accompanied by a brand new family with a whole new identity.

Secretly hidden in my small suitcase was the photo of a handsome Nazi SS officer, which would have a profound impact on the years that followed. But it was only the beginning for this thirteen year old girl - who had no preconceived idea what it would be like to live a life of secrets - forced to conceal the truth of her past.

That December I left behind that child, who during her brief young past had already lived a whole lifetime of human experiences. I left my biological family, with the lingering shame of my mother's hospitalization in a mental institution and the many unanswered questions concerning the father who had been a Nazi.

I learned at an early age that I must please in order to belong, therefore shedding my old identity - erased almost as if that part of me had somehow died or never even existed. So began the secretive "cover-up" and inner turmoil that would become a part of my everyday life - creating an even greater mystery, which surrounded the family I was born into. I lived with an inexplicable sadness and longing for those kindred souls who had to remain only as ghosts of my past from now on. I carried this burden silently within me as I was forced to live in denial of who I really was. It was not until the next four decades had passed, that the child I had left abandoned on the shore of that distant continent would eventually re-emerge feeling a powerful need to bond.

The turbulent voyage that carried me across the Atlantic was going to be the dawning of a wonderful new life in a new country. I now had a new family with a new identity, but it was also with some secret reluctance that I looked forward with excitement and anticipation to what would lie ahead. I had no way of knowing that what actually lay ahead would be more turbulence, however not the kind that is brought on by the ocean's waves, but an invisible storm which gathered slowly and silently within me over time.

Taking on a new identity reaches much deeper than merely the physical aspect. Living a life of deception meant that the truth of who I really was had to eventually surface, but for me had to "*unfold in its own perfect timing.*"

It was during one of the most difficult transitions during my life that I finally discovered I needed to connect with my past in order to find out who I really was, before I could go on. Not until I wrote this memoir did I realize that the hidden pain of my complicated past had never actually left me. I discovered that the child I had concealed for so long was still sleeping within me, causing intense emotional stress after my adoption. These recent recollections manifested into heartbreaking sorrow, and through the catharsis, I actually found myself shedding tears of compassion for that abandoned child within me.

I believe my adoptive parents never realized that denying the truth of who I had been before I became their daughter could have caused me such deep mental anguish, that the other child within me was longing to be a part of me. I never revealed those feelings of loneliness that lay hidden at the very core of my soul or allowed them to emerge. In order to tell the true story I have had to unveil some of those hurtful - often conflicting circumstances - which had been a very undeniable part of those years after my adoption; they were dominant factors which I had assumed were safely guarded beyond recollection.

Maybe through the process of writing ***The Other Child-Abandoned*** I will discover who I really am or still can be even today and once again bond with that child I had abandoned so long ago. I'm hoping by sharing my experiences I can make a difference in the lives of others who also feel a need to delve into their own past to find their "roots" or unknown true identities. We deserve the right to know the truth.

Prologue

It's December in the year 2000. Two days ago was Christmas Eve. My companion John (alias) at the time and I packed the car with all the gifts and took precautionary measures by taking along the hard copies, plus all computer discs that hold my entire eight years of work for my book manuscript.

We left Lake Elizabeth around noon on Sunday to spend the holiday weekend with my son Chris and his wife Mari in Thousand Oaks and my daughter Whendy and her nine year old daughter Miranda in Westlake Village. I also had plans to visit my nephew Kye, my biological sister Brigitte's only son.

The weather was extraordinarily warm. Strong Santa Ana winds were blowing off what few remaining leaves were still clinging to the cottonwood trees which line our neighborhood. I was filled with that glorious Christmas spirit and a sense of excitement lingered with those familiar feelings of intense emotion because I was returning *"home"*.

We took the scenic route winding through the beautiful Fillmore Valley where I had traveled so many times before years ago on that familiar two lane Highway 126 when my children were small pulling our thirteen foot trailer heading for our favorite distant camping areas.

Once again I found myself accompanied by miles of age-old orange groves and avocado orchards, their bounty sold at the family-owned fruit stands located along the roadside in front of their timeless California bungalows.

A small sign read: *"To Lake Piru"* pointing into the hills; that's where my children's father and I went on our first date when I was only nineteen. As we drove through the small town of Moorpark and came closer to the Thousand Oaks area, where I had lived the greater part of my adult life, I was overwhelmed. My chest felt heavy and the tears began to well.

Chris my son and Mari his wife awaited us at their comfortable two-story apartment nestled within a tree studded established neighborhood. The well-known fragrance that lingered in the air and the feel of those warm breezes immediately brought me back to a time I called this town my home and was very happy when my children were small. A time when my sister Brigitte and her husband Heinz were such a significant part of our everyday lives here, as a family, when Christmases together were always so special.

To my great amazement just a few streets past Chris's apartment buildings my attention was drawn to a group of trees on top of what now seemed to be left of a familiar hillside. Could this area of apartments and condominiums be the same once undeveloped location where their father and I used to hike up to what we then called *"Our Hill"* - almost forty years ago?

We dropped off some gifts and took one car to spend Christmas Eve with Whendy and Miranda in Westlake only a short distance away. Before going to Whendy's we went to the cemetery to visit the burial sites of Brigitte and Heinz and Ruby and Johnny, my former in-laws. When Chris and I compared the cards we left for my sister and Heinz, surprisingly each of us had written the same message: *"Christmas has not been the same without you...I miss you both so much!"*

I lit a candle and Chris placed a miniature Christmas tree by Ruby and Johnny's gravestone. My once special little boy has grown into a most admirable, wonderful man.

It is another difficult Christmas for Whendy. She and Drake are separated and she would like the holidays to be over. One good thing that resulted from the drastic changes in her life is that we have become closer since her separation from Drake. From my own experiences I am able to console her; only time will heal although the pain of the loss and void remains.

Early on Christmas morning Chris came downstairs to sit with me in front of their beautiful tree. We sat together in silence, hypnotized by the lights. I read his thoughts, as my own reflected back to his childhood, back to magical Christmases of long ago when innocent eyes gleamed with excitement while he and his sister watched the old Lionel train speed around our tree, which had originally belonged to his Dad as a boy.

We went to pay a visit to my nephew Kye, wife Kriste and Nicholas their son. On the way we drove the old neighborhood streets past the places where I used to shop and where I used to work. There was the Los Robles Regional Medical Center where I so often visited Brigitte during the last month of her life. Our old home on Sandberg Street looked barren without the olive trees in the front yard. I envisioned us there in the same driveway, stepping into our green station wagon as we were leaving Thousand Oaks on that chilly morning in January 1974, pulling our trailer off to begin our new life in northern California.

Kye was going through the paces of more intense chemotherapy treatments and was not feeling well, but he was in good spirits and glad to see us. I had a hard time concentrating as I was making idle conversation with Kriste's parents, delightful people who helped to keep the visit on a cheerful note.

After Christmas Kye will be staying at *The City of Hope* for a month, one of only seven patients chosen as candidates for a whole new medical procedure. I was heart-broken as I observed this courageous young man, who had lost all of his thick dark hair from the chemotherapy treatments, robbed of his promising life as he knew it three years ago.

It is difficult to revisit the past, but I will have to confront those memories and follow that path to see where it will take me.

> *"You never really leave a place you love. Part of it you take with you, leaving a portion of yourself behind."*
> *...Anonymous*

> *"...Those you love or have loved in the past remain with you forever, becoming a part of who you are..."*

> *...Barbara U. Cherish*

Chapter 1. A New Identity

In November 1950, authorities in Berchtesgaden came to Hindenburg Allee # 1, to take my 47-year-old mother, Gertrude Liebehenschel, to a mental Institution in Munich. There she would sadly live out the remaining sixteen years of her life.

After the war in 1945, my mother, sisters Brigitte, Antje and I were evicted from our home in Austria, forced to leave where we had been living after my parents divorced in 1943. Families of Nazis were no longer welcome or had any rights when the war was lost, resulting in the appropriation of our home. We ended up at the refugee camp Duerreck, in the beautiful region of Berchtesgaden in southern Germany. The camp had previously been occupied by Nazi troops during the war and was located near Hitler's Alpine retreat the *Berghof,* high on the Obersalzberg mountain.

Our mother finally located two humble rooms for us within the town of Berchtesgaden on Hindenburg Allee. It was here I had my first memories and our mother began showing signs of mental illness. Brigitte, my oldest sister, eventually took me away from my mother to live with her and the family Hutterer. My sister Antje was the only one still living with my mother at this time. Brigitte was only sixteen when she made this decision the day she found me near starvation from neglect due to my mother's illness. My father had already been sentenced to die for war crimes and had met his death at the gallows in Poland in January 1948. It was the final setback for my mother and she became progressively worse.

When they took my mother away, my sister Antje, who is six years older and I were then made official wards of the state placed under the jurisdiction of social services by the district court of Berchtesgaden. Antje was placed into foster care with the family Lochner and soon after Brigitte, ten years older, went to live on her own in the town of Furth near Nuremberg. I was then also sent to join Antje at the Lochner's. My oldest brother Dieter, born 15 years before I came along, had then recently returned from Russia after six tormenting years as their Prisoner of War.

My disruptive childhood often caused me to feel lonely, missing my parents and siblings, but I was actually a happy well-adjusted child. I had already lived in several foster homes when I went to live with Ursula and Earl Poune in 1953. They had an adorable blond and blue-eyed infant boy named Dale who soon took the place of any doll I may have owned. Ursula was the sister of Heinz, who was engaged to marry my sister Brigitte. Earl, an American who had been a bomber pilot in the US Air Force during the war, was then working for Civil Service for the European Exchange System in Nuremberg Germany, where he met Ursula. She had also been in the military service, but in the German Luftwaffe where she almost landed in one of Hitler's *Labor Camps* when she voiced her strong will and opinion why she refused to become a member of the Nazi Party.

At one point during the war she was assumed dead when she was seriously injured. The impact of a bomb had sent her flying through a window, three stories down through a 10-inch thick glass windowpane. She miraculously caught her foot on a clothes hanger, which slowed her fall before her head impacted the hard floor. Mistaken for a dead body herself, her face and body cut up, covered with glass pieces and splinters, bleeding profusely she was thrown onto a lorry full of corpses. Evidently it was not her time to go, because she saw the light at the end of the tunnel and regained consciousness. It was this same determination and strength which I would later come to know all too well.

It was Earl and Ursula's intention in the beginning to only take me as a foster child for a time, but when Earl's tour of duty in Europe came to an end, requiring him to return to the United States in 1956, they decided they wanted to adopt me. However, being forced to forget one's past is unnatural and harmful and it was during my coming of age the following years, that my longing for that abandoned child became apparently undeniable.

I was ten years old when I went to live with Earl and Ursula. The first thing Ursula did was cut off my long hair. I watched bewildered, not sure what I felt at that time, as my long thick dark brown braids fell silently to the floor and were promptly swept away; with them went my old identity.

The Pounes lived in a large housing project in Furth-Nuremberg and I liked my new home within the close-knit American Community. Each three story building consisted of spacious apartments all furnished identically by the US Army Quartermaster. Every morning the freshly baked rolls called *Broetchen* were delivered by an enthusiastic, grinning ruddy cheeked German boy who came to our door carrying the wonderful warm baked bread in a large basket.

German citizens were discouraged from entering or soliciting within the American Sector, but many who were fortunate enough to have been left with some of their valuable belongings did come to solicit, still feeling the aftermath of war and need for cash. They came to sell their heirlooms, often antiques. Ursula was a pushover for those items and she purchased beautiful porcelain figurines. Some were Hummels. She also acquired silver and paintings. Many of these things will always have great sentimental value, as I grew up around them.

One thing I admired particularly was a lighter; a knight in armor made of silver metal, he stood approximately 10 inches tall on a music box which played the popular tune of the fifties *The Third Man Theme*. I recall her bartering and dealing with the peddlers for some reasonable bargains. I always felt true empathy for these people who were forced to sell their keepsakes. She also bought a set of *Rosenthal* China and a gold trimmed blue *Cobalt* coffee service which are collectors items and now my own prized possessions.

Concealing the facts surrounding my background began soon after my arrival as their foster child. I also believe that Earl and Ursula were afraid when they started Visa proceedings that my past could possibly hinder the endorsement for my passport or entry into the United States. Ursula herself was already living a deception as well, claiming she was of Swiss nationality instead of German. Germans were not allowed to live in the project and Earl would not have been eligible to the government housing. There were some close calls when she was asked about Geneva, her fabricated supposed hometown in Switzerland, a place she had never even been. It created some very uncomfortable moments for her and her cover was almost revealed on several occasions.

Ursula and Earl enrolled me into the **Nuremberg-American Elementary School** across the street from *Gerhardt Hauptmann Strasse* where we lived. I spoke no English, but soon learned the language, which I spoke without an accent. Because of the initial language barrier I was placed back into the third grade which made me a couple years older than my classmates. That was not a problem at first because I was rather small for my age, but soon when I started to develop before the other girls in my class I felt extremely awkward. I avoided talking about the age factor, a very sensitive, embarrassing subject.

Dwight D. Eisenhower was President and schools still emphasized patriotism and pride in the flag. Songs like *"God Bless America"* and reciting the pledge of allegiance would gradually instill the love for a country I had never even seen. My new classmates and teachers warmly embraced me and as an avid reader - craving knowledge - I absorbed everything with great enthusiasm. For the 1954-1955 school year I was presented with an *"Outstanding Scholarship Award",* recommended by my teacher Miss Frances Rosenzweig. It was for an xcellent academic school record, which I suppose was quite an accomplishment for a child who could have had a definite learning disability resulting from the language barrier. Miss Rosenzweig wrote this in my autograph book:

"Best of Luck always to a happy, ambitious young lady who has such a sweet way and friendly smile!"

My name was changed from *Barbel Ulrike Liebehenschel* to *Barbara Ursula Poune* even before the legal adoption was final. My new name made every-day life easier while fewer questions arose about my background. During this transitional period in my life, I was often confused about who I really was or who I should be because I was not allowed to mention my past.

I was also converted from the Lutheran faith to Roman Catholic, taking private catechism instruction from the Chaplain Father Kapika, whose office was located within the American Army Post. At the guard station at the entrance of the American Army Post I had to stop to show my ID, proof that I was one of the American dependents. I was always relieved when they waved me to go on; somehow I feared they might find out who I really was. I was proud to be one of them and once inside the base I quickly forgot those fears and usually skipped happily along looking forward to my next lesson with Father Kapika. He was a jolly man who carried all his weight around the middle like a barrel. He had a curious habit of invariably focusing his glance at the ceiling when speaking to anyone and always rewarded me with a piece of my favorite *Bazooka Bubble Gum* at the end of each lesson.

Father Kapika was a wonderful teacher and I still have the copy of *Bible History* he gave me with *the "Catholic Chaplain's Office - HQ Nuremberg District"* stamped inside. As with all the books I ever owned, I treasured this one, especially the memories attached to it.

Ursula and Earl were very good to me and proved their love with never ending generosity. They wanted me to call them *Mom* and *Dad.*

Earl liked to order clothes for Ursula out of the *Spiegel* catalogue from the States. Weeks later after careful selections were made by him, huge boxes arrived containing beautiful dresses with matching shoes, gloves, purses and hats for Ursula. He even ordered Ursula and me a matching pink outfit and there was a pink pair of soft leather penny loafers for me. My new Dad placed a shiny penny into each shoe explaining how this was the American custom, making me deliriously proud and happy.

He had a great sense of humor but most of all he was easy going compared to Ursula who was quick-tempered and very strict. She only had to look at me in her stern, authoritative way and I felt myself virtually shrinking into the floor. Even though she often proved her very strong assertive personality, she would *"give the shirt off her back"* - still today.

They wanted me to take music lessons and went through all sorts of trouble renting a large piano that was brought up three flights of stairs by two men who looked like they were going to drop dead when they finally reached the top. It was a wonderfully given opportunity which I now wish I would have continued, but after a few months I lost interest and the piano went back down the stairs without any argument on their part. I'm sure having an instant ten-year-old daughter was quite challenging and I must have tried their patience on many occasions. That proved to be the case, especially with Ursula.

Even though my new parents provided a path to a brighter future for me, my coming of age years, especially the relationship between Ursula and I at that time, are still difficult to recall. Of course today she is a loving mother who has mellowed over the years and is not the same person she was then. During those years however, time was not always filled with carefree laughter as one would expect. It is very difficult to write about Ursula's controlling conduct. As caring as she was, little things would set her off. During those times it seemed like reigns of terror. She could easily become a screaming tyrant, forcing her restraining influence over me. Sometimes I wonder if she ever realized how it diminished all self-esteem, leaving me emotionally crushed.

I recall an incident when Ursula gave me a birthday party at our apartment. I was twelve years old and it was to be the first birthday party I ever had. Naturally I was looking forward to it with great excitement. I was allowed to invite several school friends. Ursula chose a blue dress, which she wanted me to wear. She chose all the clothes that I was to wear each morning, all the way into my high school years, and when I did dress myself I could not leave the house without her approval.

I wore my favorite new patent leather shoes and she insisted I wear one of her necklaces. David Meyers, whom I especially liked, and several other boys and girls came, including my best friend Susie Carmen. There was ample cake and ice cream, but only a few sodas. Some of the guests would have to drink hot chocolate. Ursula asked which one of these drinks each one preferred and when it came to me, I innocently asked for a soda. How stupid that was of me. I realized this as soon as our eyes met and her look could have killed me! She went into the kitchen to make hot chocolate; I followed to help, knowing that she was very unhappy with me. She was at the stove and as I stood next to her I quickly understood how furious she was when she slapped my face and angrily fumed..."*how could you be so inconsiderate?*"

I was crushed, because it seemed so insignificant, but her anger toward me lasted the entire afternoon and spoiled any further fun I might have had. I was deeply hurt and felt terrible guilt as my happy spirit immediately dwindled. I fought back the tears and forced the smiles pretending I was having a good time. The rest of my birthday party transpired in a dense fog. As I opened my gifts I barely heard what was being said and I was relieved when it was all over. I didn't care if I ever had another birthday party!

A similar thing occurred during the winter when I went Ice skating with Susie Carmen; it was in the open lot across the street. The problem was there was only one pair of screw on skates for both of us, so in order to be able to skate together at the same time we each wore one ice skate on only one of our feet. With the other foot we slid across the ice on our shoes. We slid and skated this way across the arena, giggling and laughing, holding each other up, but spending a great deal of time *sitting* on the ice just trying to get up off our back sides. We had such a wonderfully good time we hated to go home. Susie lived two buildings away and we were still laughing when we parted ways.

As soon as the door to our third floor apartment opened, an arm flew towards me and I felt the bitter sting of Mom's hand across my face. I was stunned and my happiness came to an abrupt end once again. She had been watching me from the apartment window and became enraged, *"You could have worn off the soles of the pink penny loafers!"*

Maybe those reprimands seem insignificant, especially had they come from my own parents, but not to a child who had always been an orphan passed from one strange home to another. Somehow I seemed a misfit who did everything wrong, and as before I felt I was all alone. I wondered if my own parents would have treated me this way? I found myself feeling guilty whenever I was having a good time. Once again I was sorry and would try to do better from now on.

The calm before the storm worked in reverse with Ursula. Worse even than her raised voice - which was loud enough to be heard throughout the entire building - was the silent treatment that would invariably follow, sometimes lasting a whole week. I hated leaving for school on those mornings; it left me with a sick doomed feeling throughout the whole day. I always felt emotionally destroyed when she became so angry, I just wanted her to love me. On the other hand, I knew that in all reality, she really did.

I was beginning to understand, as Dad explained to me, this was just Mom and she would get over it. I had always been shy and lived with some strict foster parents in the past, so therefore the environment of fear and respect toward my elders was not unusual for me. However no one had ever treated me like Ursula. But I could always talk to my Dad Earl, he rationalized everything and would try to smooth things over because he adored Ursula and she was so beautiful. Ursula looked like the screen actress Gene Tierney from the 1940's, dark hair and blue eyes, only the glasses Ursula wore made her look stern.

I know Earl often felt the torment of her anger also, as well as her silent treatments. Sometimes I acted as Dale's bodyguard when he was going through the *terrible two* phase. He was an adorable little terror who liked to throw temper tantrums. Often I placed myself between him, Ursula and that wooden spoon, to protect him from her mounting frustration and anger. I was more than a baby-sitter. I took him with me everywhere I went.

Everything had to be neat and clean. I learned to fold my clothes flawlessly into my drawers so the items were lined up perfectly and in symmetrical order on top of each other. If they weren't precisely even or off just a fraction, I was in big trouble. In a rage Ursula would dump out the contents of the drawer onto the floor and I had to refold everything accurately. The hanging items had to face in the same direction in the closet, no wire hangers, everything buttoned, smoothed and stretched to perfection.

I also learned how to keep a house spotless. That was achieved by wiping the furniture with a damp chamois cloth and mop dusting floors on a daily basis; carpets were swept with an old fashioned carpet sweeper. Thick white and brown cream polishes were used on the furniture once a week. Paste wax was applied to the hardwood floors by hand and polished with a heavy manual polishing brush, which was pushed across the floor with great effort, then followed with a soft cloth for the final polish. After people visited their *footprints* were quickly polished away to have things perfect.

My new Mom taught me how to make everything sparkle and keep everything spic and span, but also how to turn a house into a home. I am grateful to her for teaching me those lessons, even though often times they came with a difficult price to pay. For many years I too was a fanatic about keeping my house perfect, but thank God I have learned to relax.

The time passed quickly from 1953 to 1956. On January 25, 1956 the final adoption papers were signed by the court, by my siblings and with my ill mother's consent. Of course she never comprehended what happened to me. Ten years later she was still confused and wrote to me in a letter, *"I had given you such a beautiful name in the German language, but now I no longer have a Barbel Ulrike. How did that come about that you ended up in America? That certainly wouldn't have happened if I had been on the outside!"*

The actual adoption process was a strain for Ursula and Earl, but especially for Ursula, as all of it transpired through the German Jurisdictional System and their department of Social Services. She fought their bureaucracy and red tape, and they had never dealt with anyone as self-confident and powerful. She was not afraid to stand up to the board of investigators, looking strikingly beautiful, dressed in a black and gray suit, very high heels with a large rimmed black hat and gloves to match.

I admired her beauty, her courage and strength and occasionally even wished I could be more like her...in some ways. But most of all it was amazing because she was fighting for me, a mother struggling for her child. After they paid an unknown adoption fee I was officially theirs. Years earlier Ursula had gone through the anguish of losing an infant child. I believe that subconsciously I somehow took the place of that baby girl and I do believe that this contributed to her often unreasonable possessive behavior.

But before I was actually adopted Ursula asked me if I was absolutely sure that I wanted to live with them permanently and move to America with them. She explained to me that if I chose them to be my new parents that I would be theirs and she made it perfectly clear that I would no longer be a part of the Liebehenschel family. But of course I knew that she couldn't be serious, because I would always be a part of the Liebehenschels - that is who I was and they were my family! I did, however, want desperately to be part of a real family, and since it was impossible for any of my own to take me in, I would have gone to an orphanage. Besides, I had grown to love these people I had been living with and although Ursula was often unreasonable, it seemed they loved me too.

There would, however, be drastic changes made after the adoption as Ursula laid down some new rules. I was from now on to call my oldest sister Brigitte, *"aunt" Brigitte,* she who years earlier had always been a mother figure to me, and her husband who was in reality my brother-in-law, suddenly became *"uncle" Heinz.* It was all very confusing and caused a great deal of tension between the two families. That also became apparent when we visited my sister Antje and her fiancé Walter who lived in Wolfenbuttel.

Walter's parents invited all of us to a lovely dinner, but soon there was an uncomfortable atmosphere to spoil the festive mood. Ursula caused quite a scene when she became angry insisting I call my sister Antje *"aunt" Antje* and my future brother-in-law *"uncle" Walter.* I was experiencing contradictory feelings of happiness and gratitude for a newfound family, yet disturbing anxiety at the same time. It was a high price to pay for the luxury of belonging. I wanted to show respect to my new parents, but I also felt as though I was being disloyal to my own family. I was told that none of them really wanted me, leaving me puzzled about the truth, but much later I found out that was never the case.

It was made clear to me by Ursula that I should realize that the life and family of my past no longer existed. It was confusing and I never understood the reason for this. I don't believe that my new parents wanted to intentionally hurt me or had any thoughts of destroying my life, but that is exactly what was happening. I could never have disrespected Earl and Ursula, and therefore they never realized what they were asking of me and what a terrible burden this unnatural denial instilled. I was constantly afraid I would do or say something wrong. It was extremely difficult to deny myself the truth of who I had been for almost fourteen years. How could I disregard these people whom I had loved all of my life - with whom I had blood ties - who were all a part of me and a part of a very indisputable and unforgettable past? There was "meine Mutti" in an institution and what about my Papa?

In February 1956 I turned thirteen and received my first real kiss from fourteen- year old Nestor Rivera, who walked me home from the neighborhood movie theater one night. He was very tall, a dark Latin type, and I had a crush on him. His father was in the military and his family was being transferred to another base a few days later. It happened in the dimly lit lobby of our building and was very romantic and completely innocent, but more thrilling than I ever imagined. Could one become pregnant from kissing?... I wondered...

Mr. Sandman, Sincerely and Bill Haley's *Rock around the Clock* had topped the music charts. Elvis also came on the scene with *Teddy Bear* and *Jail House Rock* which were heard playing everywhere. These songs will always take me back to the American housing project in Furth.

A few days before leaving for the port of Bremerhafen my sister Brigitte gave me an old family photo of my parents and siblings. She quietly slipped into my room one night when I was already asleep and gently woke me. As she handed me several photos she whispered, *"I'll always love you, don't ever forget us."*

It was an emotional farewell, but when I proudly showed Ursula one of the pictures of my family the following day, she became outraged. She let me know that I had done a terrible wrong by accepting the photographs *"aunt"* Brigitte had given to me. I was given an ultimatum, if I wanted to go to America with them I had to relinquish all ties with the Liebehenschels, those people in the photograph, or stay behind in Germany. I was shattered and didn't understand her hostile reaction. I will never forget that moment when she angrily glared at me from the kitchen, looking over at me where I stood speechless and trembling in the living room. I was too stunned to move an inch.

Watching my reaction, she picked up Dale cradling him in her arms, rocking him and repeating: *"you're my only real baby"*. It was one of the most hurtful agonizing moments in my young life and her conduct was alarming. Could I ever really be loved and really belong? Feeling cast aside, alone and unwanted, I desperately longed for my own mother, who was no longer able to take care of me, locked away forever in the institution in Munich. Through my painful tears and sobs, terrified of rejection by my new parents, I hysterically cut my "old family" out of that photograph which had caused me such grief, leaving only me in the picture.

This pleased my new mother, and she wasted no time to disclose my questionable behavior to my sister Brigitte. My biological family never understood or knew the true reason behind my strange behavior but believed I no longer wanted to be a part of them. As a result, all old family ties were severed and even letters written to me by my sisters throughout the years were never given to me and I had no knowledge that they tried to make contact.

Yes, I became proficient at pleasing in order to be accepted and loved but from then on I privately held those lonely feelings within me, although sometimes that was more than I could endure.

But there was another special photo, which I would keep secretly hidden and would not share with anyone for years to come. It was of a mysterious handsome figure whose features resembled mine, a Nazi Officer wearing the black SS Uniform. Brigitte had told me he was my Papa. What was it that cautioned me to keep this secretly hidden?

Early in the month of December we left for Bremerhafen where we were to sail to New York on the *USNS Gibbins*. We traveled by train and arrived several days later. I always loved riding on trains and it was a thrill to actually experience sleeper and dining cars.

Friendly porters' wearing tight fitting dark blue uniforms and round pill-box type caps, were courteous and eager to assist us. Crisp white tablecloths decked the dining car; it was just like the trains portrayed in my favorite old black and white films.

When we first reached the seaport of Bremerhafen where the *"Gibbins"* was docked, the ship appeared ominous through the misty gray fog and cold rain - almost threatening like an enemy war ship. I remember the fascination because never before had I been this close to such a vessel.

We boarded the transport ship, our floating home for the next two weeks, cautiously walking up the long gangplank wondering how many soldiers before us had done the same. In 1944 she had carried 1000 Jewish Refugees from Italy to New York, and later she was renamed The Empire State IV serving as a training ship for the New York Maritime College.

December 1956 the *USNS Gibbins* was returning service men and their families back to the United States. I was 13 years old, accompanied by my new parents, a new three-year-old brother, facing a whole new future.

It was foggy and raining as we set sail waving farewell to the people on the dock while a military band played *The Stars and Stripes Forever.* Despite the weather, the scene was breathtaking. But as we pulled out of the harbor, I was torn by clashing emotions that overwhelmed and confused me. I felt optimistic excitement about the new country I was headed for, but a sad hesitation about allowing myself to feel happy and excited. I was leaving behind my entire past, abandoning the child I had once been. I realized I would never see my old family again, and in my mind I replayed the bittersweet scenes of my mother, my two sisters, and me - and all that we had already lived through together. I found myself leaving with a lingering shame, the stigma of my mother's hospitalization in a mental institution, but most of all the many unanswered questions surrounding the mystery about the father I never knew. But as any 13-year old, I didn't dwell on these thoughts and they were soon forgotten temporarily. Through the romantic eyes of this young girl I was about to experience a true-life adventure.

Being a military ship, it wasn't what one could call a cruise, actually far from it. However, captured through my own far fetched school-girl imagination, we were on the high seas on a beautiful sailing ship and surely the captain had to be a handsome swashbuckling pirate.

Somehow that fantasy was rudely shattered early each morning when we were awakened by the gong of the reveille and a loud voice could be heard calling throughout the ship's corridors:

"It's reveille and it's time to get up!" Each morning I grabbed my pillow and covered my ears, but soon it became a familiar routine, and if we wanted breakfast we had to jump up and get to the dining room.

I made friends with a girl my own age named Elaine. We helped decorate the Christmas trees in the ship's lounge and in the newsletter regarding the passengers' social activities it read:

THANK YOU
Have you noticed the attractive Christmas trees in the Main Lounge and Dining Room? We can attribute the decorating to:
Elaine, Barbara and Dale...

Additions and Deletions to acts and performers of the troop variety show is subject to the "rock and roll" of the good ship - USNS Gibbins!!

The ship's four page, typed newsletter *The Gibbins Express* which I have kept all these years, has yellowed with age, but the front page headlines on that December 1956, remain as an interesting flashback into history. It was written:

THE FOLLOWING PRESS BROADCAST
IS ADDRESSED TO US NAVAL SHIPS...
COURTESY OF THE ASSOCIATED PRESS...

"In Cairo the UN information's office here announced today that plans are now ready to start clearing the Suez Canal of sunken ships immediately after when British-French forces are evacuated from Port Said."

"In Moscow the newspaper Izvestia charged today that the US incited Britain and France to invade Egypt as part of a long range plan to oust them from the Middle East. It said that US policy is based on "a craving of American big business to oust Britain completely from the Near and Middle East and lay hands on all the oil riches of that area." The paper

warned the people of Asia to beware of "such diversions of American Imperialism devised to capitalize on the fiasco of an adventure they themselves provoked."

Elaine and I also spent much of our time hunting down the whereabouts of a young, blond ensign, for whom we both had developed a crush the instant we noticed him. Tall and handsome in his starched white uniform, he soon caught on to our annoying silly-girl frolics and avoided every chance that we might meet. We found out he was to be married as soon as we docked and that eventually dampened our love-sick spirits and spoiled our one-sided romantic game of pursuit.

Sometimes I explored the corridors all by myself, caught up in the excitement of what I might discover. One of those times I surprisingly came upon a large group of sailors who were as astounded as I was, wondering where I had come from? They were courteous and polite but I was uncomfortable realizing I had ventured too far. As I hurried back to my cabin, one of the sailors called after me *"In a few years you're going to be a beautiful young lady!"* Back in our cabin in the tiny bathroom, I looked at my reflection in the mirror wondering what it was they saw? After that I was more careful about my explorations around the ship.

"The rock and roll of the good ship USNS Gibbins" certainly rang true throughout our trip. The weather was furiously turbulent as we hit one fierce storm after another. The tremendous force of the huge swells battered the ship and the bridge section was partially torn off. There were rumors that this would be the *Gibbins'* last voyage as she was not seaworthy to make another Atlantic crossing. However, she would remain a transport ship until 1959. We continued to be tossed up and down relentlessly by the waves and it seemed we would eventually be swallowed up into the deep.

At such times it was difficult to walk around, so we weren't allowed on deck, but I never became seasick. I enjoyed the good food prepared in the galley, served to us at our assigned table by *George,* our friendly waiter. My new Mom however, spent a great deal of time in her bunk unable to eat anything, while my new little brother was so terribly sea sick they kept him hooked up to IV's in the infirmary.

We safely weathered these storms, but as a result of the extremely rough seas, it was a much longer voyage than we anticipated. Everyone on board was hoping we would arrive in New York before Christmas.

Finally on December 21, 1956 the *USNS Henry Gibbins*, who had once again *bound across the briny deep*, entered the port of New York and I became initiated into the *Royal Order of Atlantic Voyageurs.* We children received a colorful document pictured with sea serpents and mermaids, proclaiming our official Atlantic voyage, signed by the guardians of the deep, *King Neptune and Davy Jones.*

On deck, in awesome absolute stillness, we all caught sight of the magnificent Statue of Liberty, an unforgettable encounter sensed with unusual pride by me, even at the age of thirteen. Historic Ellis Island, called *The Gateway to America* where millions of immigrants had passed through their gates, had closed its doors only two years prior to our entry. We had to wait for several hours to come into port while the "Queen Mary" who had first priority to dock, processed her passengers to disembark. Finally we were allowed to leave our ship and immediately entered the large nearby immigration building.

I clearly recall waiting anxiously in long lines with my new parents going through all the customary immigration procedures. My new dad and brother, being American citizens, were processed through quickly while my mom and I were detained by immigration and patiently went through their routine of bureaucratic red tape. Ursula looked pale and much thinner than when we first boarded, still not feeling too well. I sensed she was nervous, keeping her red sweater jacket wrapped securely around her. I was holding on to my adorable little blond-headed brother's hand, still weak, looking bewildered and shy, yet his chubby little cheeks gave way to a faint smile as he looked up at his big sister for reassurance.

For some reason I was focusing on his polished proper little white oxford shoes, thinking he too must feel insecure sensing our apprehension. As I waited in line for immigrants I nervously clutched my German passport, feeling like an American wearing my favorite blue-jeans with turned up cuffs that were lined with red flannel plaid material with matching plaid shirt, white Bobbie-sox and brown and white saddle shoes.

But it was especially alarming and I was terribly afraid when the inspection officials asked to look through my small brown leather suitcase. I nodded, but my trembling hands were perspiring. With a great sense of relief, I observed that he barely glanced through the contents. Had he looked further toward the bottom, under the layers of clothing, he might have found an old album in which I had hidden that other very special photograph my sister Brigitte had given to me weeks earlier. The photo I had not shared with my new mother when I showed her the one of my old family. That old photo was of my father and the unmistakable design of his particular uniform carried staggering implications about the officer whose identity I would not be willing to reveal for years to come. The photograph surely would have divulged my background and I feared that I might end up rejected or even worse, sent back - deported - by myself.

After long hours of anxiously waiting and with my greatest fears laid to rest, my new family and I passed the final inspection. The process was complete and we were allowed to enter New York City. The skyline loomed in the distance, those tall skyscrapers including *The Empire State Building* of which I had heard so much about.

The first and lasting impression I had as that young girl in my new country, remain clearly defined in my memory. I was filled with intense excitement; everything seemed so vast and overwhelming, yet it also felt safe, as though I had always belonged here. Another part of me - the part I would try so hard to silence - was confused and sad. From here on out there would always prevail a quiet, secret longing for those kindred souls I had left behind and they would have to remain mere ghosts from my hidden past.

It was cold and already late afternoon by the time we took off on the New York turnpike. As we drove toward our final destination in upstate New York, my eyes followed the road with great curiosity, as around each new bend I imagined a whole new life beginning to unravel. Without any warning, it began to snow and with a sudden shiver of excitement, I remembered that it was almost Christmas.....my first Christmas in America!

"The Other Child" may have been left abandoned across the Atlantic that December, but she was always within me - sadly longing - waiting for her time to reemerge.

Chapter 2. New York

Earl's sister Florence, her husband Harold and their teenage children, who had all prepared and waited eagerly for our arrival, warmly greeted us. My new aunt, uncle and cousins lived in an old modest two story wooden frame house located in a primarily Italian neighborhood, in the town of Solvay. I quickly learned that the streets in America were not paved of Gold.

A beautifully decorated eight-foot tall Christmas tree awaited us in their front room, accommodated by old-fashioned high ceilings. Aunt Florence had baked, frosted and decorated sugar cookies in all shapes and sizes with which I especially remember we children were served chocolate milk made with *Nestle's Quick.*

There was colorful ribbon candy and traditional hard candies and mints, which will always remind me of that Christmas. Our first holiday feast was set at their large dining table. I remember the lace tablecloth and pretty china and all of the wonderful food aunt Florence had prepared.

They had two girls. The younger one, Marilyn, was my age. There were also two boys, the younger one, Harley, still lived at home. They were a typical hard working middle class family and we were welcomed into their home, staying with them for over a month while Earl and Ursula looked for a place of our own.

They were a tall lot and towered over me. Aunt Florence called me *little Barbie.* She always had a smile and uncle Harold was a joker. I soon learned what a *"Wop"* was and became acquainted with scrumptious authentic New York style Pizza. On Christmas day the house was full of extended family, people who were strangers but somehow it all struck a sympathetic cord and filled the void of those I had left behind. Even though the streets were not paved with gold I embraced America as my new home and the warmth of these loving people was a major influence, leaving a lasting impression which meant a great deal. It was like living a fantasy out of one of my favorite books, whose description of average family life in small town America, had always been of intense interest to me.

Marilyn and I shared her bedroom. White sheer criss-cross Pricilla curtains hung on her window and she had a vanity table with a pink dust ruffle around it, just like I had read about in the *Nancy Drew* mystery stories. She took down my pony tail and curled my hair into a page-boy or soft feminine curls and even let me use some of her lipstick. Marilyn was a pretty girl, fun to be with, and she introduced me to all her friends around the neighborhood as *her little cousin who just got off the boat.*

It was a wonderful feeling of belonging, almost as though I had a sister again. She took me everywhere and did not have to ask permission to go places. Before we went to the large outdoor ice skating rink she gave me a pair of her white professional looking shoe skates which she had outgrown. All I had ever had were the old screw on skates. I was overjoyed and thought I was really something skating to the music, with my hair flying in the wind like I was Sonja Henie.

We listened to the popular rock and roll music, Marilyn's favorite was *Wake up Little Susie* by the Everly Brothers, and mine was the dreamy, romantic *Venus* by Frankie Avalon. We also went to the movies and she thought nothing of speaking to strange boys who came to sit with her. It was somewhat shocking to me and I could only imagine what Ursula would think, had she known. One boy told me later it was me he actually wanted to sit with.

The days with them were happy and carefree almost as though I was a normal teenager. Something was always going on with a sense of complete freedom, unheard of in my world.

Cousin Harley, who I called a blonde version of one of my favorite movie stars of the 1940's, Tyrone Power, caused quite a concern when he decided to run away from home. After his parents had gone to bed one night, he climbed out of Marilyn's bedroom window dragging a large bag behind him. Through the tousled Priscilla curtains we watched in awe while his friend Dave was waiting for him as he climbed down the trellis where Harley fell landing with a loud crash. He made us promise not to tell. It was all very exciting and I assumed they were the typical American teenagers.

He returned home a few days later and ended up joining the Air Force. He and his brother Ronnie were my witnesses when Mom and I petitioned for Naturalization in December of 1960.

The freedom and lack of control Marilyn had in that home was something I had never experienced and I knew that Ursula was not comfortable with it. She was especially appalled when she finally did find out about our picking up strange boys in the movie theater. I had been her little sixth grader when we left Germany, but suddenly somewhere between Germany and the port of New York it could no longer be denied that I had somehow transformed into a young teenager - of course with a little help from my new American cousin. I no longer had to be self conscious of my age and hide the obvious physical changes which were developing.

With the many miles between us my family in Germany was no longer a threat to Ursula. Now in control she became increasingly more at ease since there was no more interference from the Liebehenschels. As for me, I tried to put them out of my mind, but they were always in my heart. I actually felt badly for Ursula in the beginning because I knew she was very homesick for some time. The overwhelming vastness of America was something she had to get accustomed to, as in Germany everything was on a much closer and smaller scale.

Both Ursula and Earl were hit with a major disappointment when Earl discovered that there was no position awaiting him in Syracuse as promised and the next few years were very difficult, despite his formal education. He worked several different jobs to make ends meet.

They found and rented an old house southeast of Syracuse in a great-established affluent neighborhood, in the quaint town of Fayetteville. Our home was probably the smallest, oldest most modest house within the area. To me the house was fascinating. It had a wonderful screened-in front porch and was furnished with beautiful overstuffed old-fashioned chairs, a sofa, corner cherry-wood curio cabinets and many other antique pieces. White painted cabinets beamed in the cozy kitchen with see-through glass panels, which held all sorts of pretty old dishes and red glassware. Even the refrigerator with the large motor on the top dated back to the 1930's.

We were an intimate little family and sometimes Dad would come home on special days and bring fresh donuts, including the kind he liked best, *long-johns* filled with cream and chocolate frosting. We often sat around the small kitchen table and Mom perked fresh coffee. In the cellar was the furnace and a large cistern to catch rain water where we did the laundry using an old wringer type washing machine.

But it was the attic that was most fascinating, filled with many books and old 78 records dating back to Al Jolson's time. I loved to retreat there by myself to play the thick records on the wind up Victrola and to read the old musty books for hours. It was also here I started developing an interest in the world of the 1920's and 1930's, but my favorite fantasy was living in the 1940's. I really related to a simpler life, the fashions, the homes, the cars and of course the time in history of World War II.

In my imagination this is where I escaped to, maybe because sometimes the reality was too confusing and difficult to cope with. I sang along with the records of Judy Garland and knew every word to *"Born in a Trunk"*. Here my daydreams often swept me away to that lonely place within my heart where my real parents and family would always be allowed to dwell; and they did.

I adored this amazing house and would easily get lost in my romantic world of books in the attic. Probably not the sign of a normal teenager but that was something I never felt I was allowed to be - even if I could.

The yard had cherry trees and lilac bushes and around the detached one car garage grew large bunches of rhubarb. We had "cook-outs" in the summertime on the grass lawn under the trees. Mom's sister Agi came to visit from Ohio and they made potato salad and Hamburgers. The nights were warm and humid and I can still hear the crickets chirping and see the fireflies dancing while the radio was playing *"I hear the cottonwoods whispering above...Tammy ...Tammy...Tammy's in Love...."*

Around us in contrast people lived in large two story Cape Cod style homes and rambling spread out ranch styles on large properties that had been there for years. I became known as a responsible baby-sitter and most Saturday evenings I was taking care of the neighborhood children. I liked when the people stayed out after midnight so I could watch the *Late Show* - old black and white movies filmed in the 1940's.

Catholic nuns lived within the area on a nice farm converted into a convent. Their land was surrounded by a white painted rail fence and there was a great red barn within their property. We neighborhood kids invariably hid and played in the barn, building separate rooms with hay bales for our hideaway. It was our clubhouse, but looked upon with great objection by the nuns who constantly chased us out.

The town itself was what I had always imagined a typical small town in America would look like. It had the appearance of an original New England community with a town square, a small white church with a tall steeple and main street with its businesses and quaint shops was a storybook image. There was even a corner drug store with a real soda fountain and a *cool* boy with a slick "DA" hair cut named *Jarvis* who I called *Elvis*. It was all so dreamy, just like in the old movies.

People wondered why I looked different from the other family members and questions arose about me which I didn't know how to answer. It was at that time that Dad decided to fabricate an American heritage story for me. If anyone should ask, I should tell them that I was his daughter from his first marriage, born in Oklahoma. I never really understood the actual reason behind this deception and secretive behavior, but it was done without question on my part because I did want to be accepted as their legitimate daughter.

Of course I was not allowed to admit to them, myself or anyone else who I really was. I assumed that it was probably to hide the terrible facts of my past, because there seemed to be no other reason for them to manufacture such a story.

Why was Ursula so possessive of me? But what was so bad about telling the truth of who I was and why was it shameful to be adopted? It was easier to simply submit but all this secrecy embedded deep hidden fears.

My little brother Dale didn't even know I was adopted but it was never an issue. There was a ten-year age difference between us but as far as I was concerned he was my little brother and I loved him. He was in fifth grade, many years later when I had already left home, when his Mother finally sat him down to tell him I was adopted and not his biological sister. He felt betrayed and angry that his parents had never told him. It left him traumatized and like me, he too had many unanswered questions. I hope today Dale knows that nothing could ever change the way I feel about him and perhaps through my writing he will come away with a better understanding.

I was also ashamed to admit I was born in Germany and of course it did not fit in with the story that I was from Oklahoma. However at that point in time I was only aware that my biological father had been a Nazi, but was aware that my mother was still alive in a mental institution. I don't recall at what point in time I actually found out that he had been convicted as a war criminal; it was sometime later after I reconnected with my family. Therefore, this confusing deception of falsifying my identity became a hidden but very real way of existence which was causing me great anxiety.

I often wondered about the mystery surrounding my Nazi father. Of course Ursula and Earl never spoke about it and I certainly didn't feel free to ask. Even among ourselves the lie became the reality and we never discussed the truth. Sometimes Ursula would even tell me how cute I was as a *"baby"*? "Baby"? Were they living in complete denial? Was my past too dreadful to confront? And what would the consequences have been to actually live with the truth?

On the other hand it was exactly the situation I had always dreamed of, belonging to a real normal family. But was all this deception the sign of a normal family life? By today's standards it seems very "dysfunctional". I became pretty adept at falsifying the truth and convincing people that I was born in Oklahoma, but always with the underlying knowledge that it was wrong and I was fearful of being discovered.

They were fortunately the kind of lies that did not hurt anyone but me.

Sputnik was launched by the Soviet Union in 1957 and I was enrolled in the Fayetteville-Manlius Jr. High School after passing tests, which assigned me from sixth into the seventh grade. I was still older than my class mates but I was relieved not to be placed back into grade school, because that February I turned fourteen. Aside from normal adolescence like everyone else, for me I now also had to convincingly live with my new identity. The fact that I had to keep this secret inwardly repressed was often more than disturbing. I wondered why was I forced to relinquish ties to my past? In confusion often my soul cried out to return to the child I had once been.

The girls in my school seemed intimidated by me at first, which I didn't understand. At the Nuremberg school I was a part of a large, close family, but here everything was on a much more adult level of competition. I was shy and naïve, but much more mature than my peers were in many ways. Soon they knew I was not a threat and I made several friends who invited me to my first pool party.

Fayetteville-Manlius was a rather affluent up-scale community made up of people with money and position whose forefathers were the founders of this quaint village. I found it interesting and liked the area very much, but the attitude of these people seemed very foreign. We were definitely outsiders.

Harsh winters and infected tonsils contributed to the Rheumatic Fever I contracted. After I spent some time of continuous strep throat,Ursula took me to old Dr. Weiser in our neighborhood, whose office was located in his charming Victorian home. Everything was impeccably clean and the wooden floors were highly polished. [Ursula was impressed!] It smelled of medicines and reminded me of the old *Apotheke,* the drug stores in Germany. The shelves in his glass cabinets were lined with old-fashioned medicine bottles of all shapes and his library of books and Journals looked like they were from another century. He had white hair, a stethoscope hung around his neck and he reminded me of a kind looking Santa Claus. I was completely fascinated and somehow immediately felt at ease connecting with the *old* surroundings from the past.

I began a regimen of taking penicillin on a regular basis and slowly improved. My whole body ached and I lay in bed in agony for days into weeks, which turned into months. I remember Dad rubbing my painful joints with Ben-Gay, especially my knees. I managed to keep up with my schoolwork. But I will never forget when I returned to school, being reprimanded and embarrassed by my history teacher in front of the whole class when I didn't know who, during the American Revolution had stated, *"Don't fire until you see the whites of their eyes"*. I would soon recall and never again forget that it was of course the American officer, William Prescott at the Battle of Bunker Hill.

School was fun. Our class took a field trip to historical Cooperstown, home of the National Baseball Museum and Hall of Fame. We watched Artisans at their skills of blacksmithing, horseshoeing and glass blowing. It is also where James Fenimore Cooper wrote his many novels, among them my favorite *The Last of the Mohicans*.

After eighth grade we moved from Fayetteville to suburbia, then sparsely populated Seneca Knolls northwest of Syracuse where Ursula and Earl bought a house in a new sub-division. It was one of the still booming post war housing tracts of homes which all looked the same, much like Levittown, being constructed seemingly overnight across the entire country.

Our new home was on a corner lot, one of the larger houses in the tract. The exterior was faced with pink and gray rock. Dale and I now had our own bedrooms. (We had shared one in Fayetteville.) We all helped by turning the stark new house into tastefully painted, color coordinated rooms, sometimes working until early morning hours, as Ursula never wanted to stop until it was all done. The fact I had to get up for school the following morning never occurred to her. Ursula was good at designating various jobs, but she had a wonderful flair for decorating and soon this house was a cozy home. She amazingly built a flag-stone patio along the side yard, carrying and placing the large stones herself, and soon there was a rock garden in the front with decorative pieces of drift wood, rocks and succulents.

Dad and I meanwhile put up a split rail fence around the property. He of course did most of the work, but I helped dip the railings into creosote and held them straight while he pounded them into the ground. The improvements were a family project and people stopped to compliment our pretty house on the corner of Baker Blvd. We even owned three spoiled cats. *Yatchi* and *Ming Toy* were a pure bred Siamese pair, and then there was my darling *Willie,* a huge orange striped Tabby tomcat. He used to walk me to the neighborhood A&P market a block away. Even during the severe winters of upstate New York he followed me in the deep snow.

I went to High School, bussed to the town of Baldwinsville as we lived quite a distance from town. Often we had no school on *snow days* when it was absolutely impossible to get anywhere during the storms. Baldwinsville was another small charming old New England town, but I really missed the old house and my friends in Fayetteville. Most of all I felt at a loss without the refuge of my familiar attic. Baldwinsville High was an old School. They took pride in the large indoor swimming pool which was an important part of the physical education department. I recall whenever it was time for the girls gym class to have *"pool"* instead of other sports activities, because everyone of us conveniently had our menstrual periods. We didn't like to get our hair wet as we never had enough time to make it to our next classes. The teacher soon realized the girls themselves wrote most of the excuses and she usually made them jump in. I often had a Doctors excuse due to my bad tonsils and was relieved because I really disliked *pool,* especially the strong chemicals they used in the water.

Riding the bus to school one day a boy started teasing me. He said with a malicious grin on his face, *"I know something about you and it's a seven letter word starting with an A - - - - - - ending with a D."* I was horrified and he watched me spell *a d o p t e d* on my fingers. He and his friends laughed and ridiculed me spitefully. The teasing lasted until we reached the schoolyard and I ran to the girl's restroom feeling sick. No one was supposed to know that I was adopted. I hated living with all these secrets. Thank God they didn't know of the other skeletons in my closet. From then on I went out of my way to avoid them whenever I possibly could. It seems the boy heard his parents talking about me. How did they know and what was so shameful about being adopted?

It was a time of financial hardship for Ursula and Earl. After school and weekends I helped contribute by baby-sitting whenever I could. Ursula also had a job for a short time leaving me in charge of the house and laundry. I even starched and ironed Dad's white work shirts. Ursula really could make $5.00 stretch a long way watching the newspaper for grocery store specials and buying day old bread. We ate lots of potatoes, beans and tuna, but it was always good and satisfying. She also used to whip up a delicious apple cake, much like during the depression or WW II, without eggs or butter. She sewed me some dresses made from left over scraps of material on her sewing machine, which she brought from Germany.

For my sixteenth birthday they treated me to see Jimmy Rogers performing at the *Three Rivers Inn*. It was Ursula's birthday too, we are only twenty years apart. We sat at a nice table near the stage and I felt like I was the only one in the audience, especially when he sang *Kisses Sweeter Than Wine*. He had always been a favorite and of course I was convinced he was singing only to me. It was a magical experience and I was so grateful for their loving generosity, especially since it was something they really could not afford. I truly believe my Mom had a crush on Jimmy Rogers too!

One summer we took a trip to beautiful Cape Cod where we visited with friends. Other weekends when there were no projects to work on, Earl liked to drive to various points of interest we hadn't seen and there were many in the picturesque state of New York. It was home of the historical Erie Canal which was the great passageway to the west and places like Ticonderoga, Seneca Falls and beautiful Watkins Glen. There were intriguing historical places that pictured re-creations and aspects of the life of the first settlers and significant artifacts of the Colonial and Revolutionary periods. I was extremely interested in it all.

Over coffee Earl and Ursula often talked of many things. Ursula talked at length. I listened. I am still a good listener today. However, I never divulged the undeniable loneliness or dared to talk about the void and the confusion I felt concerning the mystery that had been fabricated or the renunciation of my other family. To make things worse sometimes, Ursula received mail from my sister Brigitte in Germany, who was also her sister-in-law married to her brother Heinz. When Brigitte inquired

"How is Barbel?" [my birth name] Ursula was infuriated because my name was *Barbara,* reminding me they had paid to have it changed. Their communication and just being reminded of my family in Germany was obviously intensely upsetting for Ursula. The letters, that my sisters had written to me personally over the years, which I found out about much later, were never given to me.

I don't know why Ursula felt so threatened, but the correspondence invariably caused her great unhappiness. As for me it was so unsettling I could only retreat further within myself, denying there was a problem at all. I loved my parents, but also the family I left behind. Why could I not have both in my life? Although I tried to put it out of my thoughts it was always lingering in those secret corners of my mind. I was consumed with deep-rooted grief and like the years before when I was a young child living in foster care, I cried secretly at night, but without anyone's knowledge or complete understanding of my own sadness.

The cold war dominated America and in May 1960, Frances Gary Powers, a US agent for the defense department, was shot down by the Soviets and taken prisoner. The red scare of Communism seemed our greatest threat and had now become public enemy # 1. We also became involved in the Vietnam War in 1961, which would continue until 1976. The decade of the 1960's was also the time of the civil rights movement, anti-Vietnam war demonstrators, student protests and sit-ins, each movement demanding action, challenging the establishment. It was a time of discontent for Americans, but in my small insignificant world, things were starting to look up - at least for a while.

I was barely noticed as a freshman but by my sophomore year things started to change. Even the more popular students at school, including the cheerleaders, acknowledged me. I did have a good friend Judy - we had sleepovers in each other's homes. I also dated Dale C., one of the most popular boys in school. It was innocent, but he was my first real love. He drove an old 1940's classic coupe and was able to come visit me in Seneca Knolls. One day he surprised me with a stuffed-plush Bunny and the pop hit 45 single record *"Barbara"*. I recall I wrote Dale a card expressing my appreciation and also remember that it had to be approved by Ursula who read and censored the word "always" next to my signature. (A very humiliating invasion of a 16-year-old's privacy.) I never sent the card. Ursula was busy in her garden that day and asked him if he could pick up some more *fertilizer* in town. I was mortified because he had already delivered several large bags to her on other occasions. I believe he was beginning to feel like a delivery boy and soon he stopped coming around to see me, more than likely intimidated by my possessive mother.

It was wonderful, but painfully disappointing to experience my first real love, Dale C. I lost my appetite and quickly shed over five pounds much to my delight.

It was actually surprising that Ursula let me date him at all because she absolutely forbade me take *"biology"* or *"sex education"* in school. She had a confrontation with the school principal and much to my embarrassment I had to transfer to other classes. The day she saw me reading *Little Women* she was appalled, her temper flaring once again, and made me return it to the library. I tried to explain to her what a fine piece of literature it was, but she was convinced it was some sort of sex novel. I recall Dad and me looking baffled at each other and he just shrugged his shoulders, never standing up against her outrageous behavior and demands.

My badly infected tonsils were a persistent problem for me and I missed a great deal of school. I continued taking the penicillin prescribed by the doctor until I was faced with a near death experience from an allergic shock reaction. I remember taking the tablet as I had done so many times before, when shortly thereafter I felt myself losing consciousness. I was able to call to Ursula and Earl who were out in the yard and the next thing I remember was looking down at myself lying in Ursula's bed. Strangely, I was floating up at the ceiling and from above the room I observed a doctor and my frightened parents at my side. Ursula was crying and I really didn't understand what was going on. Then suddenly I was back in my body hearing only faint voices talking to me. They seemed to come from somewhere off in the distance.

Ursula gently stroked the wet hair from my face and Dad looking relieved said, *"Where've you been tootsie?"* I was pretty frightened and so glad to be back to familiar surroundings. It was a Sunday and fortunately the doctor in the neighborhood was not golfing as usual. Had that been the case, there would not have been enough time to administer the life saving antihistamine. From that point on it was no more penicillin for me, as even to be in a doctor's office where someone had been injected with the drug would cause me to react with frightening symptoms.

I had a tonsillectomy at age 17 and my health improved. Unfortunately, all these absences from school would be the deciding factor leading to a particular circumstance which still haunts me to this day.

Hal and his wife Rita, a girlfriend from Mom's bowling team, lived with us for a few weeks. Rita had black hair, big blue eyes and a gorgeous figure. I thought she was the most beautiful woman I had ever seen. I always admired black hair, as it reminded me of my sister Brigitte. Rita was a few years younger than Ursula and I found it very easy to talk to her. She obviously saw that there was a problem within our home and that I was unhappy. I never told Rita that she was my mentor at that time, a tremendous influence in the life of a lonely and troubled young girl. Suddenly there was a breath of fresh air and the house was full of fun and laughter. I remember she planned a wonderful afternoon which took us swimming to a reservoir and how much I relished the adventure of our picnic - stretching long into the moments of twilight that evening. I watched with interest while she cooked in Ursula's kitchen preparing her special pasta dish with bell peppers and garlic. I admired her pretty ankle bracelet and she showed me an exercise that helped keep her pretty legs in shape.

Before we left Syracuse for California she said to me *"Barbara, just remember that if the time comes that you can not handle your problems, there are doctors who can help you."* I recall looking at her very puzzled and completely startled for suggesting such a thing, because I didn't think she knew about my real mother in the mental institution. I wondered, did she think there was something wrong with me? I found out her reason for that statement sometime later when she wrote to me:
"I felt that eventually you would have more problems within the family. I knew that your mother ruled the family and also remember how tough she was with Earl. I always felt the one who got off easiest was your brother Dale. I most of all remember that she treated you more like a maid than a daughter which always confused me. I remember how unhappy you were and I certainly understood why when

I saw how you were treated. To be as possessive and dominating as your Mother, is a sickness and you suffer when someone fights your possessiveness. I saw her faults when we lived together, but these faults did not affect my life so I continue to like her."
                                        Rita Kricks January 6, 1965

That summer at the end of my sophomore year we rented a cabin with some friends along one of the beautiful lakes of Onondaga county. Before we left for the cabin I had received a formal invitation to a membership tea given by the chapter of the *Sub Deb Club* of Baldwinsville High School. This was an elite organization much like a sorority and they invited me to *pledge* in the fall. Needless to say, my days at the lake were made up of excitement and daydreams, while enjoying the barbecued home made kilbasa sausage made by our polish friends the Paninsky's. I will never forget and can still hear Mr. Paninsky singing his favorite song while cooking the sausage, *"Put your sweet lips a little closer to the phone..."* They were nice people with whom we shared a fun and memorable time that summer. All these dreams, however, quickly faded the first day back at school in my Junior year.

Due to my illnesses the absences had become more frequent while my self-confidence had dwindled, bringing with it alarming feelings of anxiety. Today I distinctly recall sinking deeper into a state of confusion and anguish, living a lie and concealing the truth of my secret past. The absences only added to feelings of terrible insecurity and fear, knowing I had fallen behind after yet another bout with illness each time I returned to school. My parents were unaware of my emotional despair.

As a result of the absences I lacked sufficient credits and now in my junior year I was horrified to find that I was assigned to a sophomore homeroom. This was especially humiliating and extremely traumatic for me because I was already older than the other students. I was terribly embarrassed and devastated. I went home very upset, and crying I told Ursula and Earl I didn't want to return to school. I was shattered, having always liked school, and even though I had skipped a whole grade and had been a good student, I fell behind due to my illnesses.

Today I often think how easily that could have been remedied with some supplementary tutoring. It was never suggested that I see a counselor who surely would have told me then that it was not the huge problem I perceived it to be. I needed guidance, but Ursula and Earl agreed that I could drop out of school. I know as parents they felt sympathy for me but to this day I wish someone could have helped me make better choices for the well being and direction toward my future.

Earl promised I could still get my diploma and go to a Jr. College. Of course that never happened. My friends tried to talk me out of it but nothing could have made me return at that time. To this day, forty years later it is still regretful and often in my dreams I am seventeen again walking the halls of Baldwinsville High School or it is in the present-day and I am there to receive my diploma. Perhaps some day I will.

As a result my high school years are not particularly of pleasant memories, adding more regrets and yet another dark secret to my already hidden past.

I knew, however, there must have been a reason that I was sent back into my body when I was so near death. But now at age seventeen it seemed the whole world and surely a brighter future was awaiting me.

In December 1960 Ursula and I proudly became Naturalized American Citizens. Cousins Ronnie and Harley stood up for us in front of the court as our witnesses.

There actually were exciting things about to happen in the very near future. Dad had taken a job at the Veterans Administration in southern California, leaving us behind to sell our house. The prospect of moving to California was happening at precisely the right time. My personal reasons however, were unlike those of my parents. Perhaps this could be another new beginning. Perhaps with even more distance in between, I could more easily ignore that *"other child"*.

However, the suppressed "Other Child" within me always yearned to be acknowledged and chose to surface while I lived through those difficult teenage years in New York in a state of depression. I didn't understand it at the time and I don't believe anyone ever knew the terrible burden I carried all alone.

Chapter 3. California

In the early spring of 1961 I had already turned eighteen when Earl returned from California to pick us up in Seneca Knolls and drive us across the country to our new destination. He had many exciting stories to tell about the wonderful life in southern California and brought Ursula and me matching west coast style *Capri* pant outfits. The house had finally sold and the movers had already come and gone. Our large light blue station wagon was packed, I had several books to read and we were ready to leave on our long road trip across the United States. As with previous phases of my life, this was to be another thrilling adventure. I looked forward to seeing the many states we would have to cross and of course they even wrote a song about the famous *Route 66*.

Even though it was enjoyable and there was much to see, it was a tiresome trip, especially for Earl who did most of the driving, often into the night. Ursula made sandwiches and we frequently ate in our car. It was with great appreciation when we finally stopped overnight in a motel and were able to shower and I could wash my hair.

One of the most memorable sights that left a very profound impression on me was Albuquerque, New Mexico. The vast clear blue skies, the red earth and sand and authentic native Indians wearing their colorful ponchos and large hats, was completely fascinating. I had only seen that in the movies and both Ursula and I were totally amazed - while the desolation of the vast Texas panhandle was surreal.

At a lonely gas station, in an adjoining shack where the proprietors apparently lived, a young boy was peering at us through ragged curtains, which were swept up and flying in the hot desert wind. He came out staring at me through the open car window in silence. I will never forget that pathetic look on his dirty little face. *"Do people really live like this in America?"* I asked my Dad. It was very enlightening and I was in awe of this country, which demonstrated such extraordinary contrasts geographically as well as economically. I thought to myself that everyone needed to take this kind of road trip throughout the United States and see what the heart of this country is all about. Through the waste lands, miles of deserted straight roadways stretched ahead of us and seemed to meet the horizon at the end with nothing but a mirage reflecting off the hot pavement. I read my books and time passed.

We arrived in California in about a week and rented a furnished apartment in Canoga Park in the San Fernando Valley. Dad returned to work at the Veterans Administration on 1380 S. Sepulveda Blvd. in West Los Angeles.

We all adored the bright warm sunshine which greeted us with the sweet fragrance that came from the orange groves and the open spaces of undeveloped land that was still to be found in the Valley at that time. The colorful Oleander and Bougainvillea bushes fascinated me and of course the tall Palm trees too. The sides of the freeways were covered with *Ice Plant,* a green succulent ground cover that bore white cactus-like flowers. This intriguing type of vine seemed to grow everywhere in California at that time. I was very conscious of the natural beauty around me. We looked up some old friends and they showed us about Knott's Berry Farm, Farmers Market and Hollywood. I knew this was home!

At our apartment, it seemed every day, Ursula sent me to borrow the vacuum cleaner from the managers, as our household belongings were still in storage. After a whole week of this routine these people became very annoyed and I told Mom it was embarrassing and I didn't want to bother them any more.

One day as I was taking our trash to the Dumpster behind the building I spotted a book with a worn blue cover that had been discarded. Books were precious to me and I usually cherished the older ones even more. Quickly retrieving it, the faded title read, *Gone with the Wind* and I felt as though I had found a valuable treasure. From then on the time that transpired at our San Fernando Valley apartment evolved entirely in my fantasy world of Civil War Atlanta. My new friends and heroes were Rhett and Scarlett, Melanie and Ashley, and for a short time the beautiful southern mansion *Tara* became my new home. I was completely swept away by my imagination.

Even though I liked California, I would much rather have lived in this fantasy world of the past. Ever since the days I was consumed by my favorite books in the attic in our old house in Fayetteville I longed for a simpler time and really didn't like or feel as though I fit into this life as it was in the present. I suppose that was an escape taking me to places far away from the secrets I was hiding which were too difficult to face, but unfortunately impossible to forget.

I was so caught up in that book that I really don't remember much of anything until we moved to Thousand Oaks. This sleepy little community was nestled among golden rolling hills and lots of gigantic old oak trees. About one hour northwest of Los Angeles, it was a very small town of less than 3000 people at that time. I didn't know it then, but Thousand Oaks would be my home for many years to come and even today I feel a warm heart-felt connection for this region.

Many new housing tracts were just going up in this growing area. One of them even boasted a *fallout shelter.* Our house on Calle Jazmin was in one of the original housing tracts in the *Conejo Valley.* [Rabbit Valley] They were modest three bedroom homes on large parcels of land. Ours was a smaller parcel backed up against a wall of solid rock and adobe soil. Ursula tried to cultivate and plant this hillside without much success, but finally some *ice-plant* took hold. The house came with *wall to wall* carpeting, a *country kitchen* and again Ursula was happily making this house into her new home.

California would be an education for me in many ways. There was much more going on than actually met the naked eye and what appeared on the surface to be the perfect lives of these people who lived in suburbia. Across the street the woman waved good bye and sent her man off every morning blowing him kisses, only the man in the blue truck was not her husband! A few houses down the street a couple with several children had a secret of their own. Our neighbors on one side of us were two very friendly guys. Mom told me they were *gay.* They were not called *gay* in those days, but it was definitely something very new to me. Life here in California seemed much more relaxed than on the more conservative East Coast.

On the other side of us lived Mack and Paulette, a very young couple, not much older than I was, with two small blond-headed adorable children. I often baby-sat for them and became acquainted with some of Macks' college friends. All of them were *Political Science* majors and were products of the *Beat Generation, which* soon would give way to what became known as the *Hippie Generation.*

Paulette didn't know how to keep house, cook or even take care of her babies. Often I found them lying in wet cribs with diapers that hadn't been changed for hours. I felt sorry for these darling little children and when I babysat they were bathed and well taken care of.

Mack and Paulette invited me to one of their parties and introduced me to *Rose* wine while we sat around on the floor on pillows in a trendy *beatnik* fashion with candles burning in Chianti bottles, listening to Andre Previn music and Ella Fitzgerald records. We discussed the controversial current futuristic film *"1984"*. It was all about how *Big Brother* controlled the world. They must have had premonitions of the *World Order* we are becoming so aware of today. We had interesting conversations and I was growing up, but still it was a time of innocence.

There were wide-open spaces all around us giving the impression of the old west. Within walking distance from our housing tract was a western movie set and often Dale and I went to see them film *Gunsmoke,* a popular TV series of that period. Along the dusty trail tumbleweeds chased us and lone gourds grew out of the arid adobe soil, their long green fronds bearing huge white blossoms which seemed to reach out into the barren badlands. It all stirred my vivid imagination as well as my love for the old west, and it could not have been more intriguing.

There were actually many actors and movie stars living there at that time. Eve Arden, Vera Miles and Joel McCrae had ranches near by. I often saw the tall handsome cowboy stroll around town wearing his familiar ten-gallon hat. He was married to the beautiful actress Frances Dee and I frequently saw them in the Mexican Restaurant *El Tecolote* in the town of Camarillo.

Walter Brennan lived in the small near-by town of Moorpark where we bought our fresh meats at *Spencers Market*. In later years he befriended my brother-in-law Heinz, who became and was the manager of *Spencers* for years. The actor Kurt Russell also lived in the area as a child.

The original town consisted of one main street lined with numerous buildings starting along the old Ventura Boulevard which eventually turned into Thousand Oaks Blvd. heading west. This road was originally part of the El Camino Real where stagecoaches used to travel this Highway on their routine trips from Los Angeles to Santa Barbara. Thousand Oaks was also home to *Jungleland,* the park like animal compound consisting of Elephants, Lions, Chimpanzees and more. It was here that the young son of actress Jane Mansfield was brutally attacked and mauled by one of the lions, sometime during the 1960's.

There were many charming old structures making up the town center, among them the Rock House Restaurant, built entirely of rock and the original Oakdale Market. There was also Harold's House of Omelets which still exists today. The old A&W Root Beer drive-in was one of the last of its kind which still employed the soon to be forgotten car hop waitresses.

The most famous however was the wonderful Eddie Kover's Redwood Lodge. This landmark was once a stagecoach stop. Huge Rock Pillars supported the upper level and a tall Cigar Store Indian sat in the front to greet the customers. The Restaurant was on the first floor and the second level had rooms to rent, which were said to have been occupied by ladies of the night in the past. The adjoining group of small Motel Bungalows was used as location sets in the Oscar winning film of the late 1920's *It Happened One Night,* staring Claudette Colbert and Clark Gable. Unfortunately fire destroyed this landmark and most people today who occupy the newly constructed office buildings will never know about the wonderful old lodge which once stood on this site. A couple miles from Thousand Oaks, in Newbury Park, was one of the few remaining outdoor drive-in Movie Theaters.

Ursula made friends easily in the neighborhood and some of the women suggested that I enter the *Miss Thousand Oaks* Beauty Pageant that May. I really did not feel particularly comfortable about the idea, as I was extremely shy, but it was a good chance to meet some girls my own age. Ursula was acquainted with the owners of *The Meadowbrook Plunge,* which was a public swimming pool and picnic area, who voluntarily became my sponsors. The pageant photographer took the official photos required and he told Ursula that I was very photogenic and reminded him of a young *doe.* He didn't know that my nickname used to be *Bambi.*

The preliminaries were actually quite fun. We did many promotions and our pictures were in the newspaper showing us in front of a different business every weekend. A brand new *Sizzler Steak House* had just been built on Thousand Oaks Blvd., which we helped to advertise. Being one of the chain's originals it was complete with sawdust on the floor and huge Texas cattle horns for wall decorations, all very befitting our charming western town. We were in the local parade and from the back of an old pick up truck we waved until our arms ached. Together with my friend Marty , who worked for the Thousand Oaks Answering Service, we contestants learned how to walk straight and turn gracefully, taught to us by teacher June De Spain, owner of the local modeling and dance school.

It was a fun way to make many new friends and the activities helped me get over some of my shyness. I came to know what a *box lunch* was, made by us contestants and then raffled off to the highest bidder. The local boy who bought mine later told friends he thought I was *stuck up.* He of course couldn't have known that I hardly spoke to him only because I was painfully shy. Ursula always told me not to act too eager and it was better to play hard to get! I came away that day thinking he hated my tuna sandwiches.

Ursula took me shopping for a white *Catalina* one piece swimsuit and my formal dress was a pretty pink hand-me-down, which had to be altered, but actually looked quite stunning. I was only 5'3" tall, but most of the other contestants were not much taller. I was told that even though I was small, my figure was well proportioned and I should be proud of my 18 inch waistline. A friend who was a beauty consultant applied my make up and piled my long chestnut brown hair on top of my head. The other girls complimented me, but of course they all looked radiant.

The event took place at Jungleland on the Lions' stage where they surrounded us in their cages. Most of that evening transpired in a haze, but I do remember when it was my turn to walk out on center stage, the emcee questioned me why I had entered the contest. Then, without any warning, my nervous response was drowned out by the unanimous deafening roar of the lions. I received an enormous applause with enthusiastic laughter coming from the audience and I could not have been more relieved that the lions voices took over for me.

But most of us girls didn't have a chance because the beautiful statuesque six foot tall Francene obviously won the crown. But looking back, this was the least important part of the whole experience and no comparison with the large organized beauty contests of today. We were all genuinely happy for the deserving contestant. There seemed to be no bitter competition between us and we all went away having learned an important lesson which was about friendship and camaraderie.

The fun I had leading up to the actual pageant was without a doubt the main event. Soon thereafter we would all go our separate ways; as for me, I seldom even recall that I actually participated in a "Beauty Pageant".

It would be 20 years later that my memories would fondly recall this time, when my own daughter entered the same contest. She was striking and most beautiful. I believe it was Heather Locklear who won that pageant in 1981. Those roaring lions on that stage at Jungleland are only a small segment of personal memories symbolizing the old town of Thousand Oaks which will always hold a very special place in my heart. Of course progress and the passage of time have transformed the community, but I wonder how many people remember it as it was then?

Our neighbor Mack introduced me to Larry who drove a dashing white *Austin Healy Sprite* sports car. He lived in Granada Hills, but came out to the *Conejo Valley* every weekend to spend time with his friends our neighbors. There was a whole group of nice young people who assembled regularly; many attended San Fernando State College. They were a fun crowd and we would often go to Zuma Beach. Larry would speed through Decker canyon, a treacherous winding road that ended up at Pacific Coast Highway, which runs along the Beaches into Malibu. He was what they then called a *Ho-Dad,* a surfer boy, and we were a perfect example of the popular Beach Party scene.

I delighted in the unique sound of the *Beach Boys* singing about *California Girls* and quickly learned to love the West Coast as I sat on the Beach while Larry rode the waves on the incoming surf. It was one of those days I saw the handsome young actor *Ron Ely* on the beach. He walked by and smiled at me showing his deep dimples. I thought my heart would stop beating! At that time he was currently starring in the hit TV Series *Malibu Run.*

Larry was the typical California Beach Boy of the 1960's! We played at *Pacific Ocean Park* where we rode the huge roller coaster, which seemed to be speeding out into the water. I sampled Margaritas in a nearby quaint little Mexican Cantina. I'm not sure how I was served, but the Margaritas tasted wonderful and probably would have even without the tequila. Everything was a new exciting experience for me.

Several of us went to see a comedy in some well-known Playhouse in downtown Hollywood. They were all laughing, but even though I didn't really understand the sophisticated humor I laughed along with them. I certainly was learning lessons on adulthood, but I couldn't help my reaction of complete shock and surprise after the guys had gone to Tijuana, Mexico for a weekend and Larry told me that Mack, who was married to Paulette, had slept with a Prostitute.

My friendship with Larry never graduated to a serious relationship, but we had fun together that first summer in California. My Dad, however, had a problem with Larry, and unfortunately the primary reason being that he was Jewish. Just as with Gays, religious or racial prejudices were never an issue with me, but they always were for my Dad.

Although I kept it tucked away in the farthest corner of my mind there was a very definite *Jewish issue* for me when I dated Larry. I often thought of the fate of his people during the war and the terrible secret I was harboring. Although I never knew him, the guilt of who my father had been was always there to haunt me. It disturbed me immensely, but of course no one, including Larry, knew of my well-kept secret past..

My first summer in California was about to come to an end and I was ready to go to work. Earl helped prepare my resume declaring more fabrications. I was apprehensive, but he assured me I had nothing to worry about. It seemed my whole life had been contrived and based upon deception. Earl had already falsified other legal records, which I never understood. As far as anyone was concerned I was born in Oklahoma. But it only confirmed to me at that time that my past was something I should never talk about. Some years later I asked Ursula why they hid the truth about my past, but she could not give me a valid reason.

I answered an ad in the local newspaper for a position as a dental assistant. At that time it was not required to be certified and no experience was necessary. They would do the training. Ann, the office manager, called after the interview to inform me Dr. Case said I had the job as his chair-side assistant.

The office was within 20 minutes walking distance from our house, located in a nearby housing tract. I did not mind my daily walk and every morning I admired the world around me enjoying the California sunshine, but most of all the freedom. The housing tract was located within a better up-scale neighborhood where the dental office was situated in an addition built adjoining the doctors' home.

I learned a great deal throughout my almost two years as a dental assistant. I came to know the name of each instrument and was trained on all procedures performed in the office, working hand in hand assisting the doctor. I had to set up a tray for each patient according to their individual dental procedure and was responsible for the cleaning and sterilizing of the instruments. I didn't take the x-rays, but it was my job to develop them in the dark room. I also kept the bathroom and waiting room clean and straightened and did such a thorough job of cleaning the bathroom one day that toxic fumes sent all of us, outdoors including the patients, gasping for fresh air. I had poured bleach and another chemical cleaner into the bowl at the same time, which created a dense suffocating fog throughout the entire office. Dr. Case wasn't too upset with me, but I was certainly embarrassed for such stupidity on my part. Dr. Case was a pleasant man, a sort of father figure, but a bit temperamental at times which I was told was the criterion to be expected of most doctors. We worked well together and I really enjoyed my job, although it was quite demanding and consisted of long days and hours on my feet.

We were like a close family within the office. Dr. Cases' wife often invited me to have dinner with them at their home on those nights when we worked late, usually due to emergencies. One of those times I had a bit of an emergency myself when I rinsed the utensils and instruments that had contact with some penicillin the Doctor had been using without my knowledge. I immediately felt the allergic reaction, but they quickly gave me some antihistamines to counteract the penicillin.

I was making $42.00 dollars a week. My first pay-check was spent on some badly needed clothes and shoes. Up until now many of my things were hand-me downs or even Ursula's clothes altered to fit me. I was so proud to be able to buy some skirts and blouses at *Sally Shops* and some matching hi-heels from *Gallenkamps Shoes* located at our new local outdoor shopping center **The Janss Mall**. It was an incredibly proud feeling to have real money in my wallet, which I had actually earned myself. Finally I had something of my very own and my first taste of independence.

I also wanted to do something very special for my Mom and Dad to show my gratitude for all they had done for me. Ursula had been dreaming of a new living room set and that was exactly what I wanted to buy for them. At McMahans Furniture in the town of Oxnard we were assisted by a smooth talking salesman named Jim . He was my age - rather cute with a charming southern drawl. He helped me to open up a charge account in my very own name. My gift to my parents included a three piece Sectional Sofa, a kidney shaped two-tier coffee table with matching end tables. It would be an affordable monthly payment and I would still have money left over.

I believe I was as thrilled about this as they were. Jim came to see me several times wanting to take me out, but I never went out with him. He subsequently did television commercials and our paths would cross again years later when he once again used that southern charm to try to sell a car to my husband. He told me then, *"Why you're just as pretty as you ever were!"*

Dr. and Mrs. Case had a young son and also an older son in college. When Greg came home on a school break we went out on a date in his father's Porsche. We went to see *Flower Drum Song* at Grauman's Chinese Theater and afterward walked on Hollywood Blvd. In a small shop I spotted a print of a *Keene* painting. I loved Keene's work, whose subjects had exceptionally large eyes. He bought it for me saying it reminded him of me. We had a good time, but he soon left to return to school.

I was seeing less of Larry and occasionally dated other boys. One of Mack's friends, Jerry, who I had often seen at his house, asked me out. He was tall, blonde and very charming. We were really just friends and the whole time we sat on top of Mullholland Drive in his VW Beetle looking down at the twinkling lights below, he talked of his girl friend in England, and I listened. He kissed me that night on Mullholland Drive and although it was nice it was without sparks or fireworks. We both knew it was only a friendly kiss.

One of the most exciting things to happen while I worked as a dental assistant was the time Dr. Case invited me to go to a dental convention with him. We had to drive to Los Angeles and it was an all day affair. I met his colleagues from the USC dental college alumni and was introduced to many young professionals. I sensed that I seemed to make a good impression and Dr. Case was pleased and played the part of a proud Father. Their talk of Boats, Planes and country club memberships certainly engaged my attention, especially when I was invited to go flying with a very nice looking Doctor.

I felt like I was the Bell of the Ball that day and came home breathlessly telling Ursula of my most exhilarating experience. She listened, but only heard half of what I was saying because she was lying on the Sofa suffering with *morning sickness.*

I did date one of the young dentists I met, following the convention. Dr. J was interesting and good looking and of course Ursula and Earl liked the fact he was a professional, but we soon stopped seeing each other when he found out I was Catholic. It seems the Catholic religion had caused serious problems in a prior relationship of his. Coincidentally the song *Moon River* by Andy Williams was popular then, always a reminder for me of the very nice Doctor J.

It was autumn when Mom and Dad found out they were going to have another baby. My reaction was peculiar and maybe even shameful, but I was horrified. Outraged, I told Mom *"It should be my turn to have babies now!"* I'm sure it's not what she wanted to hear, but within myself I knew the real reason for my reaction. I didn't tell them but I was afraid I would be the one responsible to take care of this child. I remembered years earlier when Dale was small, how I was depended upon to take him everywhere with me, or stay at home to baby-sit. That seems to be the way it happens within all families; the older ones always take care of the younger siblings. Ursula had a tough time the first few months and almost lost the baby, and it was to be a difficult pregnancy both physically and emotionally, and also for me. They called it a "change of life baby".

The following thirteen-year cycle - which lay ahead - would be one of the happiest of my entire life. It was also a time when I was able to reconnect with my past.

Chapter 4. Love, Marriage and Children

I met Dave (alias) my future husband in February 1962. I had not turned nineteen yet. At work Ann sent me across the street for some donuts. I had to walk through the waiting room. A nice looking guy in his early twenties was sitting there reading a magazine, he looked up and we both said hello. Behind me, I felt his eyes follow me out through the door. When I returned with the donuts, Ann was taking his x-rays and I then proceeded to take him into a room. He was about 6' tall with blonde wavy hair and large blue eyes.

He had a nice smile and there was a comforting aura of self-assurance about him that I liked. What impressed me most about him then were his highly polished loafers and his Ivy League button down shirt tucked into neatly pressed slacks with a most perfect crease that could have only been brought about with heavy starch. He said, *"How come I've never seen you around?"* I answered *"I don't know?"* He claimed I said *"I don't care!"* and years later he still swore that's what I had said to him on that first day.

He told me his parents lived in Thousand Oaks; they had come to California from Iowa during the war. His father had worked on the secret bomb project in Los Alamos, New Mexico and they had lived in San Fernando on the corner of Devonshire and Balboa, then still open countryside, but today it is a busy intersection. I also found out later that his parents, who had been recent patients of Dr. Case, told him of a *pretty new dental assistant* working for Dr. Case and he should make an appointment to see for himself. That was the reason for his visit to the dentist. He told me he worked offshore on San Nicholas Island for the Department of Defense and he flew home only on weekends.

When he left that day I checked the scheduling book and already looked forward to his next appointment, at which time he asked me out for his following weekend at home. I could hardly wait for the week to pass. I worked Saturdays with Sundays and Mondays off while he flew in on Friday evenings, weather permitting, and returned to the Island early Monday morning. Some weekends he was stranded on the Island when the weather kept them grounded and I found I missed him.

We were soon spending every Saturday night and Sunday doing something together. We both loved nature and preferred to do things outdoors. We had what we called *Our Hill*, an undeveloped area within the outskirts of town that has long been replaced with condominiums. We hiked to the top with a blanket and underneath old Oak trees we spent wonderful private afternoons just getting to know each other and enjoying the pastoral beauty and serenity of the golden hillsides around old Thousand Oaks.

We had picnics at Lake Piru and Lake Sherwood. The latter was a beautiful undeveloped natural lake surrounded by the wilderness of *Sherwood Forest* consisting of age-old oak trees. Unfortunately, progress has turned this area into another planned community for the wealthy with large homes sitting where we used to have our picnics in the Forest. It brought tears when I recently drove through this area. Somehow I have a difficult time accepting change and progress, wishing things could remain in their natural state, as they once were long ago.

Dave was the most mature, responsible person of his age I had ever met. He had made Sergeant in the army where he spent three years at Fort Ord near San Francisco. He then went to work for the Navy as a civilian hired recently at the Pt. Mugu Naval Base. He worked in the Radar Section of the Department of Defense and in later years he would be part of the expansive Missile Program. He earned a good salary and was paid per diem for staying on the Island.

He owned a 1957 Candy Apple red Chevy convertible and a beautiful sleek red Pontiac Bonneville Sedan. He had a boat and enjoyed water-skiing. He had also bought a parcel of land for investment purposes in the *Greenwich Village Tract* off Thousand Oaks Blvd. Dr. and Mrs. Case also owned a parcel there and they were very impressed how responsible Dave was at such a young age.

But it wasn't the things he owned or the money he made which impressed me. He was only twenty-four and I admired his incredible strength of character and stability. He treated me with loving respect and I felt safe and secure when I was with him, knowing he wanted to take care and protect me. He had a strong willed personality, but he was a good man and exactly whom I needed at that point in my life. My Guardian

Angels had sent him to me. I can't say it was love at first sight, but it didn't take long for me to fall in love with him and it was wonderful having those weekends together to look forward to.

I also came to love his whole family like my own and they embraced me like I was already a part of their family. His parents Ruby and Johnny lived on Montgomery Rd. in Thousand Oaks only a few blocks from Calle Jazmin, and our dates often included them just barbecuing in their backyard. We danced in the moonlight on their recently poured patio that had *sparkles* added into the concrete and we necked in the back seat of Dave's classic *1937 Nash,* which was parked on his parent's property. Ruby was an excellent cook and she baked the best pies and I give her much of the credit for my own culinary talents as she taught me many basics. His sister Sally (alias) lived in Palo Alto and his Brother Ron (alias) was to be ordained as a Catholic Priest that coming May. Needless to say by Easter of that year Dave asked me to marry him - I said yes.

But before I could consent to marrying him or anyone, I had to confess the terrible secrets I was concealing about my family. If I told him that my mother was in a mental institution and my father had been a Nazi, would he still love me and want to marry me? I agonized about this until I could wait no longer to tell him. Tearfully I related everything about my past and about being adopted. It was the first time I had ever talked about these things with anyone and it was difficult to actually get it out and put into words.

He listened with compassion and afterward with tears in his own eyes he just held me close to him and from then on he was not only the man I loved and would marry but he became my best friend. It seemed like all of my fears simply melted away.

Dave's strong personality often contradicted Ursula's and they actually only tolerated each other. Dad wasn't too fond of him either and usually sided with Ursula to keep the peace. On those days when Dave came home for the weekends I always had to confront my Mom as she made trouble for me about seeing him. After dinner on Saturday night before I could go out with him it was expected of me to clean up the kitchen and do the dishes after I came home from work, even though I seldom ate with them on those nights. The delay seemed agonizing and somehow cruel and I could hardly wait to leave the house to see Dave after being apart the whole week.

On Mondays when it was my day off it was the normal routine for me to help Ursula clean the whole house. Sometimes Dave would come home on Mondays when he was forced to remain on the Island over the weekend, but since I had the house to clean I was not permitted to see him. Johnny, Dave's father whom

I adored, wanted to give me driving lessons and came to pick me up on one of those Mondays. He saw me scrubbing the kitchen floor on my hands and knees. I was terribly embarrassed and humiliated to have to tell him that my mother would not permit me to go with him because I had to clean the house. I'll never forget the disappointed and puzzled look on Johnny's face; he told me later, he thought I was treated like Cinderella.

Neither Dave nor his parents could understand that kind of behavior and were very angry with Ursula for the control she had over me. It all added to the rift which came between my parents and me, a wedge which would gradually cause us to drift further apart- while I grew closer to Dave and his family.

Before Dave's mother Ruby even met Ursula, she said, *"I don't even know your mother but I hate her already."* I had learned that Ruby always said what she thought, but nevertheless the ugly truth was very upsetting. Regardless of what had transpired I didn't want people to think badly about Ursula and felt protective because she was after all still my Mom and I did love her.

Ruby's harsh conclusion was regarding the particular instance when Ursula absolutely forbade me to attend Dave's brother's ordination ceremony into the Priesthood. Oh, how I wanted to go; it would have been such a special experience. However, later I was allowed to attend Father Ron's first mass in China Lake, where their family had lived when they were children.

When we became engaged, Dave wanted to give me the beautiful ring he had chosen alone in privacy on some special romantic evening.

Ursula, however, had other ideas of how that should be done. She wanted to give an engagement party and told me at that time Dave should formally propose to me and place the ring on my finger in front of both parents and all of our guests. She said this was the German custom. I had never heard of it. Although I appreciated the thought of her giving us a party, I was very unhappy about this intrusion of our most private moment and Dave was appalled at the idea. Still, we did as she asked hoping to keep her appeased.

It turned out to be a very nice party if it hadn't been for an uninvited guest. Larry suddenly showed up, and with total disregard, he appeared unconcerned in his usual cut off surfer shorts and sandals looking like the beach bum that he was. Mom gave him the cold shoulder, Dad was rude, and I uneasily tried to explain it was my engagement party while Dave wanted to punch him and throw him out of the house. It was definitely bad timing on Larry's part and also the last time I ever saw him.

After the party Mom and Dad criticized Dave because he did not wear a tie to the party. That seemed like such an insignificant complaint when he tried so hard to please them and most important I had found someone who really loved me. The staged marriage proposal did nothing to improve the strained relationship between any of us.

During the week we sent letters back and forth to and from San Nicholas Island. Dave wrote:

"Dear Barbara

Well I am out here on this rock once again and right now I can't even think straight. I wish I could tell you in words just how much you mean to me and how much I want you to be happy. Until I found you I didn't know what the word love was or meant. Since you came into my life and heart, I can't stop dreaming of you.....

With all my love.. Dave...Monday [6pm] June 16, 1962

We set October 20th for the wedding date and Dave gave me a book on *Sex Education* knowing how naive and inexperienced I was. I didn't dare take it home even at this point of my upcoming marriage. But

I wasn't concerned. I knew I would learn soon enough. Dave, however, studied the book and learned about *the rhythm method* of birth control. Precise at this as he was about everything he did, he had the exact method down to a tee and I later became pregnant only when we planned it.

I also had to go to confession so I could receive Holy Communion on our wedding day. I never attended church although I had my own faith within my heart. I was terrified of going to confession and beside the fear I didn't even know how. Dave wrote down for me what to say to the priest and gave me a small pen sized flashlight to take into the confessional so I could just read it off the paper. I will never forget this experience as long as I live. As I closed the door behind me, the confessional became pitch dark. The Priest asked when my last confession was. I told him *"Never!"* as I nervously fumbled for the flashlight. When I turned it on, the small cubicle I was in and also the other side where the Priest sat, lit up like a stage. Mortified I heard the Priest gasp and clear his throat and I vaguely heard myself reading my speech off the notepaper. I did get through it and survived the embarrassment and everyone had a good laugh about that story later, especially my new brother-in-law the Priest, Father Ron. I still have the note, from which I recited, within that illuminated confessional on that day long ago in 1962.

It was also the last time I ever went to confession. The priest who heard my confession was the same one who gave his consent to our marriage, but asked Dave when he interviewed both of us, if he wasn't *"robbing the cradle"?*

There were many developing circumstances that would make the following months and the years thereafter even more troublesome for me. The difficulties began at home and often I was so upset that the people at work became aware and wanted to know what was wrong. I couldn't tell them the actual reasons but they knew of Ursula's pregnancy and realized what a difficult time she was having physically as well as emotionally and were very supportive.

One of the most traumatic events at that time was the fact that Ursula's brother Heinz - who was also my brother-in-law married to my sister Brigitte in Germany - came to live with Ursula and Earl. He was planning on working in America for a brief time after which he planned to return to Germany. He was still *Uncle Heinz* as far as Ursula was concerned and suddenly all the confusing family problems of the past came back once more to haunt me. She seemed satisfied however as long as I called him *uncle,* still living that lie, denying my past. But how could I now avoid the reality? I was no longer a child; I was 19 years old! I remember the morning he arrived. He came in to wake me - still half asleep, I laughingly told him to *"go away!"* pulling the covers over my head. But it was wonderful to see him, just to know he was a part of my sister Brigitte. It didn't take him long to see what the situation was at our house and we often talked, but he was only a third party and Ursula was his favorite sister, which placed him in an uncomfortable position.

She faithfully drove him to his job at *Jungleland* every day, regardless of her morning sickness. It was a whole new line of work for Heinz who took care of the wild animals in the park. He learned the language and seemed to like working outdoors, soon boasting a great California tan. The only thing he complained about was the never-ending tuna Mom served so often but it was always done with a great sense of humor.

Gale was born to Mom and Dad on June 29th. She was a darling chubby red headed cherub. Now they would have another little daughter, as soon they would give me away in marriage.

My mother-in-law and sister-in-law to be gave me a beautiful bridal shower and a friend planned another. We received many lovely gifts and necessities. I was so very proud and thrilled to have my own things and could hardly wait to set everything up and play house in my very own home.

Dave and I were busy making plans for the wedding, he was saving to buy our furniture. Always sensible and practical he wanted us both to save and combine some of our income so we could pay cash for the items needed to furnish our apartment. That would have been fine but how could I tell him the truth? As a result of my secrecy he became very angry with me and we had our first serious quarrel. He couldn't understand what I was doing with all of my income.

When I could no longer avoid it I finally had to confess to him. As the result of Ursula's puzzling silent treatment of me after I was hired at my new job, I found out she expected me to help the family. Since this subtle coercion and the terrible guilt feelings on my part I contributed my earnings to my parents.

Again he was very upset with my parents, especially when he found out about my furniture payments. He felt they should take them over once we married but that of course was not the arrangement I had made. The loving gesture, which I was so happy to bestow onto my parents, seemed to cause nothing but aggravation and trouble between Dave and me.

We bought all new furniture at a local discount store and a week before our wedding around Dave's 25th birthday we had it delivered to our brand new rented apartment on Calle Quebracho on the second floor. When they set up the bed and placed the mattress we both looked at each other reading each other's mind. We didn't move in until after the honeymoon but it was a wonderful exciting time and we laid in each others arms on top of the bare mattress dreaming of the time we would share this bed as husband and wife. We would wait but the anticipation was almost too much to bear at times.

Dave paid for my beautiful wedding gown. It was custom designed by me with a full hoop skirt just like Scarlett O'Hara's out of "Gone with the Wind". It was like every girl's magical dream come true only this groom took the responsibility to pay for most of the wedding. He ordered and paid for the invitations. We chose to include the names of both parents, which didn't make Ursula very happy. He also paid for my red Roses and the other flowers and corsages and also generously paid for Ursula's specially designed dress and matching shoes which coordinated with the brides maids' dresses.

We were married in the old Catholic Mission Church in Camarillo as Thousand Oaks did not yet have its' own parish at that time. Father Ron, my new brother-law, performed the ceremony. He told me later *"I knew my brother was hooked the night he went out to warm up the car for you!"* It was an especially beautiful emotional ceremony. I cried throughout the whole service. It was not a large wedding as only about 50 people were invited and fewer attended.

Our reception was at the lovely home and garden of the Burnette family of Moorpark. They graciously opened their home and offered the use of their beautiful china and silver. Mom made little tea sandwiches, Dad prepared some type of Punch and Ruby contributed a turkey she had roasted. Dad worked with Mr. Burnette at the VA and his two young daughters were my bride's maids. Dave's pretty red headed sister Sally was my maid of honor. She was only three years older than I was and we hit it off from the very beginning. She was my new sister with whom I could let my hair down and even get a little crazy sometimes.

Dave's best friend Don was his best man and Boyce was an usher; he knew them both from the army. I had met them and their wives a few months earlier, the weekend Dave and I flew to San Francisco so I could meet them before the wedding. They became very dear to me and have remained my best friends although both Don and Boyce are now gone.

People suspected I must be an exceptionally sensitive and emotional girl to shed tears throughout my own wedding ceremony. Although they were also happy tears, I never told anyone that there were other reasons for the emotion, that there were deeply hidden thoughts which carried me far beyond to another side of the world, back to another lifetime.

My thoughts were of the people from this former life who couldn't be there with me on this special day. No one knew I had another mother, one who was locked behind walls and gates, all alone in an institution, a mother – meine Mutti - I was supposed to have forgotten about long ago. She was someone who had to endure so many adversities in her life. How I longed to have been able to make it up to her. How I wished she could have been there with me to hold me and wish me well and take part in the festivities. How wonderful it would have been if the *Papa* portrayed in the photograph, which my sister had given to me so long ago, could have given me away, and if only my sisters and brothers could be here with me today. All these facts had made my life so complicated, but I was actually so fortunate to have two sets of parents.

Ursula and Earl were unmistakably proud of me that day and no matter what had occurred between us in the past I loved them more than ever on my wedding day, especially when my Dad Earl gave me away as his daughter. I was glad that Heinz was there as a representative of the other side of my family. He would soon return to Germany and I would feel alone once more missing him terribly. But now I had Dave and finally for the first time in my life I knew I really belonged to someone.

When I was changing out of my wedding gown into my blue going-away dress, Ursula handed me an envelope. I read the card with great emotion and I knew she was watching my every reaction. The card was signed *"With much Love on your Wedding day, from your sisters, Brigitte and Antje"*.

We left our guests at the reception and drove to Bakersfield stopping the first night at the Bakersfield Inn. We were so anxious to get away that we left the marriage license behind. Dave's brother, Father Ron, brought it to us that night to our motel. I don't know which one of us was more embarrassed. He later teased about our inhospitality and how we actually left him standing outside the door without even an invitation to come inside!

Any couple's wedding night has to be a beautiful memorable event between two people, but it was especially moving and exceptional in our case as it was the first time for both of us to be intimate with someone. We had both wanted to wait. Starting tonight we belonged together forever and of course I knew this feeling of happiness could never end....or could it?

Dave had everything arranged and we honeymooned in Yosemite National Park. It was wonderful in our cozy cabin all alone. The autumn colors were spectacular and we explored the entire valley hiking and riding bikes to the lakes, mountains and waterfalls. At that time they still demonstrated the *Firefalls,* a weekly event when a huge bonfire was pushed over the edge of the rock which I believe was *Halfdome,* a breath-taking experience. It will always remain one of my favorite parks.

There was, however, a little black cloud that invaded our happy solitude and that was what had actually transpired in the world outside at that time. It was those days in October that became known as *the Cuban Missile Crisis* and Dave was afraid he might be called up for the Army reserves. As it turned out, fortunately that disaster was avoided.

On our way back home we stopped to visit with our friends Don and Betty, Boyce and Mary Jane in the San Francisco Bay area. I heard Dave tell Don, *"You have to watch out for the quiet ones!"* followed by roaring laughter.

I was actually anxious to get back to Thousand Oaks to set up our apartment and make it into our home. I couldn't wait to play house with the pretty new things that had been given to us and to cook my first dinner for my husband. I was deliriously happy and loved being married to Dave. I wanted to be a good wife and prove to him I knew how to keep a nice house and wanted to improve my culinary skills. I even starched all of his shirts the way he had become accustomed from his days in the army.

When it was time for him to fly back to the Island leaving me alone in the apartment during the week, I was grateful to have my job to return to. I didn't have my driver's license yet, but drove our sleek, long red Pontiac to work only a few blocks away from home. The first time I went to park it back into its space between two poles in the apartment garage, I scraped the right side going in and repeated the procedure as I tried to straighten it by backing out. Dave's pretty car now had an ugly dent in the side. I was very upset.

We didn't have a phone yet and after dark I ran up the block to the near-by *Country Cousins* market on Avenida Los Arboles, crying all the way there. I was almost hysterical when I asked for change for the pay phone outside of the store. After many transfers from one department to another I finally reached Dave. Sobbing, I related what a terrible thing I had done to his beautiful car. I felt so badly, but all Dave said calmly was *"I guess we'll have to get a smaller car!"* And a smaller car we did get; it was a red *Corvair.*

Dave was the one who had given me driving lessons which no doubt gave him some premature gray hair. I almost ran into the fence at the newly constructed Thousand Oaks High School and probably gave him a bit of a whip lash when he yelled *Stop!*...of course I did as he told me to and immediately put on the brake. I failed my driver's test twice, because twice I had the infamous merciless gray-haired driving examiner of Oxnard whom everyone dreaded. I stalled in the middle of a busy intersection and he told me I should have used my choke...but my car was automatic? The second time I was so nervous I failed again, but finally passed on the third attempt.

Our friends living right below us at the apartments were Ted and Ann, also newlyweds with whom I was able to visit when I needed someone to talk to. I'll always remember the look on Ann's face when I came to retrieve the ice cream we had stored in their freezer. Blushing sheepishly she confessed *"I'm sorry..I ate it!"*

Sometimes Dave's sister Sally came into town and visited with me at the apartment while Dave was on the Island. We listened to *The Four Freshmen,* my favorite vocal group of that time and the beautiful crooning voices of Vic Damone and Robert Goulet. We were like two schoolgirls together having the time of our lives in my very own *Pad.* She married Don the following February and I was her maid of honor.

I relished the freedom I now had, but it also became more difficult to carry on an amiable family relationship with Ursula and Earl. I really wanted to see them and share my life with them, but there was tension between us, as Dave always felt unwelcome. The truth was Ursula still had that hold over me causing Dave concern and frustration. I felt I was pulled in all directions, but worse things were yet to come.

The deception and denial which I had been living for almost ten years was to suddenly reemerge in all reality in the spring of 1963, as Heinz, my sister Brigitte and their ten year old son Kye immigrated permanently to America. When Heinz had returned to Germany, he became desperately *homesick* for America. They dissolved their entire household and moved to Thousand Oaks to make a new life. Ursula and Earl were their sponsors. I was ecstatic at the thought of having my oldest sister near me again, but also realized this would definitely create some major problems within the family. I recalled the unpleasant scene back in Germany in 1956, the controversy that had driven me to cut up my family's photo.

The questions I pondered were soon to be answered. Ursula gave me another ultimatum before Brigitte and Heinz even arrived in Thousand Oaks. She let me know that I now had to choose which one of them I would recognize as my family. It was either Brigitte as my *aunt*, denying that she was my *sister*, or I was no longer a part of their family. That was some choice and it manifested into extremely frightening and very visible emotional distress for me. Again I was faced with those confusing options which seemed so completely unfair and unreasonable, when all I really wanted was to be happy about all the beautiful things which were occurring in my life.

I welcomed Brigitte to America, our reunion was emotional and tearful as we hugged and clung to one another. I embraced her as the beloved sister that she was and vowed that day, that nothing and no one would ever keep us apart again. Brigitte had told my sister Antje in Germany before she boarded the plane, *"If Barbel calls me 'aunt' I will return on the next flight!"*

Dave and I planned our first child and in April of 1963 she was conceived. I immediately experienced symptoms of morning sickness and quit my job as a dental assistant. Shortly thereafter we bought our first house in Camarillo, which was about twenty-five minutes from Thousand Oaks. Together with our friends Ted and Ann we moved into our new houses on Jay Avenue. Ted and Ann were also expecting a child and had bought a house with us on the same day within the same tract - down and across the street from us.

Our husbands left us alone in our vacant houses while they loaded our things into a trailer back at the apartment. Ann and I, both pregnant, miserable and hungry, devoured the sandwiches that Ted's mother eventually made for us with some peanut butter and bread she found in a lone grocery bag. Our homes were located in a brand new tract, nestled among farmland and walnut groves. We purchased it for $18,500 with a $90. down payment, for a nice three bedroom two-bath house that had bare tile floors, a great kitchen and a good sized backyard.

I was welcomed into my new home by the *Welcome Wagon*. A friendly lady with a basket full of merchant's coupons and brochures introduced the newcomers to the area. We would live there for four years before moving back to Thousand Oaks.

Dave soon left San Nicholas Island landing a job back on the mainland at the Naval Base at Point Mugu. He came home every evening, although he would work the night shift for some time. We did many improvements to our little home. Dave beautifully landscaped the whole yard and as always, in the most precise fashion. He first drew out plans which placed every shrub in its' location, although we did not take into consideration that they would eventually grow in size. In the backyard the *pampas grass* bush planted next to the house soon covered the entire bedroom window. Dave even built a waterfall from decorative rock, which we hauled from Grimes Canyon. He stowed some homemade beer he had made in the storage section inside the structure and we soon heard explosions when the caps popped off under pressure. It was something he tried only once. He was not a big drinker at that time, but it was a fun activity for him and it was actually very good tasting beer.

Dave sold his *Greenwich Village* parcel and with the proceeds we bought carpeting to cover the barren floors. He converted our garage into a *rumpus room,* a lovely family room that he enclosed with paneling. He laid some pretty tile across the entire floor which I kept polished with paste wax, like Ursula had taught me to do years ago. The garage door was left in tact so it could still be opened, but it was concealed with weather stripping covered with paneling on the inside. He was a proud homeowner and did beautiful handy work. We bought our first color TV and watched *Bat Man* in beautiful living color. However, the black and white series *Peyton Place* was my favorite as well as the old films which I will always cherish.

I will never forget and remember clearly that sad day in November 1963. I was seven months pregnant wearing a green maternity outfit. I was ironing in my living room in front of the TV, when the emotional Walter Kronkite announced that our President John F. Kennedy had been shot and killed in Dallas, Texas. Dave and I tearfully watched the televised funeral and of course the salute given by little John-John bidding his father farewell, left a heart wrenching impression on all Americans.

In the meantime our daughter Whendy was born to us on January 11, 1964. It was a difficult delivery and after more than eighteen hours of hard labor she was born by Cesarean section, something almost unheard of in those days. My very concerned doctor was Don McGillis, the father of the talented actress Kelly McGillis. He was a wonderful caring doctor and held off on the surgery until he had no other choice. My allergies frightened him, as we had had a scare in his office one evening after hours. Someone had previously received a penicillin injection in the same room and it resulted in a violent reaction for me. He stayed with me attempting to keep me stabilized while he sent Dave running frantically to a pharmacy for some *Nutra-pen*. He almost lost me that night and I became a somewhat special patient to him.

As I laid in labor at the small local Conejo Valley Community hospital on that windy night, they administered some morphine and once again I started to go into shock. Dr. Don was speechless and after those incidents he knew why I refused to take drugs of any kind.

Whendy Jeannine was a beautiful pink angel with lots of black hair. I received a dozen red roses from her proud father who still looked sick with worry and anxiety. I brought her home to her lovely nursery a week later, which we had freshly painted and decorated months in advance. A second-hand crib was the main attraction, which we had repainted and trimmed with decals surrounded by a swag canopy which I had sewn of sheer soft yellow material. I had continually saved my *blue chip stamps* for a bassinet, toys and other items. There were tiny outfits and lots of cloth diapers ready and waiting, all gifts given at the baby shower my sister Brigitte had planned for me.

Before Whendy's birth I often spent time in her room in wonderful solitude just admiring everything. I wondered at those times, if my own mother had ever experienced those kinds of moments when she was expecting me. It was only recently when I researched my book, ***The Auschwitz Kommandant***, that I discovered my arrival was not a happy time for my parents and soon thereafter my father left my mother for another woman.

Dave and I frequently wrote each other little notes. He left me this one when Whendy was only a month old. There was a large heart in the center with an arrow drawn through it.

February 11, 1964
Hi My Baby,

I'm just sitting here with a cup of coffee, trying to think of a poetic way to tell you how much I love you and need to be loved by you. It's such a beautiful feeling to know that you love me and don't mind doing those monotonous jobs day after day. Well it's time to go, I'll call at 12:30 or so.

Love you so much, Dave

Life continued in Camarillo. Those were still the days of *the milkman*. Chase Brother's Dairy delivered bottled milk to our front door, which had ample rich cream at the top. He also offered other products like cheeses and eggs. I looked forward to *Jewel Tea* , that friendly man who always had some special items, which he brought into the home in a large basket. Their own brand of Jell-O and spices were of exceptional quality. Each purchase earned points and with them I received a pair of red wool slacks which were a favorite in my wardrobe for many years.

The *Fuller Brush* man was a nice older gentleman who became a friend and our Life Insurance agent, Mr. Emery, came to pick up our monthly annuity payment, while he sat chatting, enjoying a cup of coffee, filling us in on the latest news around town. The *Helms Bakery* and *Good Humor Ice Cream* trucks, however, were the all time favorite of the neighborhood children as well as our own. I fondly recall the large banana splits Dave bought for us on hot summer days. What great traditions these door to door salesmen were in our every day life and what wonderful memories they bring back.

Among those simpler times were the special days when I hung Whendy's cloth diapers all straight in a row on our clothesline in the backyard. It was very tranquil, almost therapeutic when they were swept up by the whisking wind, left with the smell of clean fresh air and even folding them was somewhat of a ceremony.

Whendy was diagnosed with a *congenital hip, which* meant her hipbone had not properly developed. She had to wear a brace from three months on until after her first birthday - which kept her legs aligned to correct the problem. She was amazing because it never stopped her from crawling, standing and even walking before she was a year old.

It was also a time of getting reacquainted and reminiscing with my sister Brigitte and her family. Heinz had returned to the job he had left at Jungleland and from there he was sent to be head caretaker for several months at the famous San Francisco Baby Zoo.

Brigitte took off alone on her first road trip, one she would never forget. On the radio they were playing the popular tune of the time *"If you're going to San Francisco be sure to wear some flowers in your hair"*. She delivered two small chimpanzees and a hyena, driving from Thousand Oaks all the way to San Francisco with the chimps in her back seat jumping up and down in their cages. The hyena was kept in a large cage in the open trunk secured with a rope. Frantically, the hyena tried to chew its' way out of the cage, but was finally subdued by the carbon monoxide. Brigitte had only recently learned to drive and those two noisy chimps and the screaming hyena in the trunk did nothing to soothe her nerves along the busy highway.

She was emotionally distraught and terribly embarrassed when she received bewildered looks from people whenever she stopped to refuel at gas stations. When she and the animals finally arrived at their destination at the San Francisco Zoo the hyena recuperated, just needing some fresh air. Brigitte, who wanted to see Heinz in San Francisco, however later wished she hadn't volunteered to transport these primates and the hyena to the Baby Zoo. She was very courageous, but then she always did what was necessary throughout her whole life, always considering others first.

Almost immediately after their arrival from Germany Brigitte started work at the *JJ Newberry's Dime Store Cafeteria*. I still see her wearing the little yellow and blue Dutch uniform, just doing a lot of smiling. She hardly spoke the language, but was soon hired by *Semtech Electronics Corporation* in Newbury Park where she would remain for the next twenty-five years.

After a period of six months at the Baby Zoo in San Francisco Heinz decided he wanted to return home to be with his family. He was then hired at *Spencers* Market in Moorpark and became their Butcher and Manager until he retired. They had rented before they finally bought their own home on 2850 Calle Damasco, an opportunity which would never have been a possibility in Germany. The *Spencers* catered a wonderful housewarming party for them in their lovely new home. For me this home and the presence there of my sister, Heinz, Kye and their dogs was a sanctuary of security, a safety net for over twenty years. It represented the warmth of family memories not only on special holidays but a lifetime of everyday human experiences for all of the family both happy and sad. Happy memories like the morning before we all left for the airport for our trip to Germany, we met in their kitchen toasting champaign to our anticipated good times.

We saw our children grow and change throughout the years as we all did, depicted by each new picture added to Brigitte's photo album. Together at this home we encountered birthdays, weddings, funerals and an incredible family closeness we all knew and share still today if only within our hearts. Brigitte and Heinz thoroughly enjoyed having a yard of their own and we had many back yard barbecues together, playing games like croquet and badminton.

My nephew Kye came to spend a weekend with us in Camarillo when he was still a young boy. I recall his fascination with my pressure cooker. He told his Mother in amazement how good and fast it cooked a whole pork roast. Kye was an only child somewhat lonely and spent a great deal of time with his cousin Dale, my little brother who was only two years older. Soon Kye was a great help to his parents especially around the yard. He initiated many projects such as building brick walkways and planters, always responsible like his own father, and so unlike most of his peers.

The confusing circumstances of our family ties did not stop us from becoming each other's best friends and we always had fun times together. Sometimes we even were a little crazy. I recall the day we wanted to send our sister Antje in Germany some *unusual* family photos. I painted big freckles on my cheeks and blackened out one of my front teeth, puffing on a large cigar. These pictures showed that our lives were not always somber. Those were the times Brigitte often talked to me about our family and writing a book herself, but even then the subject of our father was treated very discreetly. I wish I had asked more questions, but I believe it was at one of those times together that she explained to me that our father had been sentenced to death for his involvement at Auschwitz.

I was very proud of my home and family and my domestic existence at that time. I tried to give my two children the love and security, which I had missed during my own childhood. I felt it was very important to instill the basis of a close family unit, especially the warmth of a mother who was always there for them. I actually felt like I grew up with my children in many ways, doing all the things children like and need to do. On our black and white TV, together we watched *Captain Kangaroo* and *Hobo Kelly*. They were my *Christopher Robin and Winnie the Poo* and on those *"Blustery Days"* I relived my childhood through them when they played house under the dining table, covered by sheets and blankets.

However, the relationship between our family and Ursula and Earl was becoming more strained and we drifted further apart. My Dad Earl sent me some letters, which he wrote to me starting December 1963 through November 1964. I have kept them all in their original envelopes with the 5 cent stamps still on them. These are excerpts starting with the first letter he wrote in 1963. They explain what was happening during that difficult time after my sister came to America.

December 31, 1963...
"Dear Barb,

 This is a difficult letter to write but write it I must. I have wanted to talk to you for a long time. I realize you are probably puzzled at your mother's hot and cold attitude, frankly it sometimes throws me a curve but I have figured it out. It's an emotional situation that has been building for a long time and I am afraid that if it doesn't come to a head soon, she is either going to wind up in Camarillo [state hospital] or go off the deep end and do something for which she will be sorry for.

 I don't know whether you realize it or not but your mother has a very deep love for you. I had hoped that this emotional impasse would gradually be dimmed by time, unfortunately it has become more intense to the point where I fear for her sanity as the least little thing will set her off...not the noisy steam blowing kind but the quiet ones.

What set her off after Christmas was seeing your birthday card to Brigitte. It took me two days of prying to find out she now feels you care more for Brigitte then you do for her. I have talked myself blue in the face for some time trying to convince her that this is not so...but you know your mother's stubborn head. I know from talking to Brigitte that things are not like Mamma imagines but the thick headed Kraut in her stymies everything.

I realize you probably think why don't I do something about the situation, well, I have two small children to worry about and I have to sacrifice some things I believe in to maintain a relative stability in our house...and it ain't easy.

The one thing and person who can completely cure the situation is you Barb, all you have to do is get on the phone [call collect] and say Mamma I need you. I'll guarantee you will see a changed woman who will knock her brains out for you and Dave and the baby.

After this letter came I did go to see *Mamma* and I let her know how much she meant to me. Our relationship resumed, but as hard as I tried it was never the same. Something else would always set her off and there was no easy cure as Dad hoped there could be. I would not give up Brigitte as my *sister* and Ursula could never accept that fact and frankly I became tired of the constant friction.

Dad's letters continued....

July 7, 1964

Many thanks to you and your sister for breaking the family apart. Your sister should be real proud, it took her ten years but she successfully split you away from us and her husband away from his sister. Heinz said it was all your mother's fault. I got wise to your sister when I would hear the statement "doesn't Brigitte have a lovely sister". It was quite obvious

*she wasn't telling these people, who we were mutually acquainted with,
that we were your parents?*

July 30, 1964

   *Truthfully you and Brigitte have much more in common then you
have with Mamma and I, what with a blood relationship and similar
physical and mental characteristics, our relationship was merely on paper.
We forgot about characteristics you inherited at birth which could never
be changed.*

November 4, 1964

   *Truthfully you ceased to be our daughter from the time you first
fell in love with Dave...oh yes Barb it was obvious to Mamma and I even
in those days that we had become secondary.*

November 17, 1964

   *It is difficult to throw away ten years of love and devotion and
even though Mamma gives it lip service, down deep inside she is hurting
that is why she's pulled the curtain around herself. How do you end an
era? With a letter like this? It is difficult to say, a reply would be useless.
I can see both sides of the picture, which you and Mamma can't.*

   *Someday if Whendy asks about her Grandparents you won't have
to be embarrassed explaining about us...since you can tell her the truth
about her real Grandparents!....*

                              ...All my Love, Daddy

   With the last letter Dad included the family photo he had kept on
his desk. It was of him, Ursula, Dale and me taken at Christmas 1956 and
held such fond memories of when we had first arrived in New York. He
had some new pictures made of *the family* he told me. That last statement
he wrote inferring the truth about my real parents was by far most hurtful.
But I never held the letters against him, even though they did deeply hurt
me. Always before he had been the one I could depend on and go to when

things bothered me, but I knew he himself was tormented and had to lash out at someone. We still saw each other off and on after that last letter.

My mother, who had lived in the Institution in Munich for sixteen years, died in June of 1966. I knew she had been ill and I was able to send her some flowers and get well wishes. We had also been corresponding after Whendy's birth and she wrote me a very sensitive moving letter. I recall her loneliness that could be read between the lines especially one sentence in her letter which she underlined, *"When will we see each other again?"*

I remembered sadly the few years I had lived with her during my childhood and the many things we had gone through together in that short time and how I missed her after I was taken from her. It was a sorrowful homecoming from our long planned camping trip to Oregon that June when I found out about my mother's death.

Our son Christopher Duane was born on September 23 of that year in 1966. Dr. Don McGillis was still my physician and he informed me it would be another C-Section. Two weeks before the scheduled delivery, at the time of my check-up, I found out his brother Jim had taken over Don's practice. Jim was very nice, but I was very upset. On September 23rd Dr. Don came all the way from Redondo Beach to assist in the delivery, actually just to be there to hold my hand. I have never forgotten that kindness and dedication. Since I didn't have to go through any labor, the recovery was much easier this second time. But I missed being away from my little girl. Whendy was not allowed into the hospital, but I recall Dave held her up so she could see and wave to me through the window. In later years she would recall when she saw me through the hospital window.

Chris was my bright bundle of joy with the biggest brown eyes, which I know he inherited from his grandfather Arthur Liebehenschel. Chris was a happy baby, but he had severe allergy problems. Eventually we put him through a series of tests and a ritual of injections. We had to rid his surroundings of all possible dust, turning his room into a complete sterile environment. His stuffed animals were packed away and his carpet, mattress and curtains had to go. Dick built a special bed and we purchased a thin mattress, which we placed into a plastic cover. His asthma gradually improved with time and today he can eat almost all of the things he was formerly allergic to.

Whendy was two and a half when Chris came on the scene and she experienced a definite case of sibling rivalry, a little jealousy problem concerning this new brother with whom she now had to share her parents' affection. On several occasions she acted out her insecurities. She meant well when she fed him some raisins, on which he almost choked. But her baby brother was very unhappy when she decided to bite into his little foot. The day she tried to smother him with a pillow I fortunately just happened into the room! My little pink angel had a definite mind of her own.

Whendy was four when we sold our house in Camarillo and moved back to Thousand Oaks. We could have had a little trouble selling this house as Whendy proved true the saying, *"Out of the mouth of babes."* Her room was a soft shade of pink with pretty pink shag carpeting and white with gold trimmed furniture including a canopy bed. She resentfully watched the people looking through her bedroom and told them *"This room has a crack in it!"* She was referring to the baseball that came crashing through her window one day. We had some explaining to do to the prospective buyers!

We rented for a short time and that is where we spent a day in complete anguish when Whendy had wandered off before we finally found her playing at the neighbor's yard behind us. Soon afterward we bought the house on the hill on *Camino Del Zuro.* It was a lovely much larger home than the one in Camarillo. The real estate market was in a slump and we were able to purchase this *fixer-upper* for a reasonable price. It was in the *Tara* tract, an upgraded neighborhood, and Dave knew he could make all the improvements.

Of course this was not Atlanta, but I was sold on this *"Tara"* home. It already had nice landscaping in the front yard, lots of Ivy on the hillside with a beautiful pink blooming *Mimosa* tree surrounded by green lawn. Under that lovely tree the kids and I often had our own little picnic lunch of sandwiches and lemonade.

Dave did all the backyard landscaping, pouring a huge patio that ran the length of the house and another smaller one at the corner of the yard situated under two existing full-grown eucalyptus trees. We adored that house and used to sit under the trees enjoying the view. It was here that Chris rolled down the sloped driveway in his stroller. Dave, taking giant steps, ran through the ivy stopping the run-away stroller before it reached the street heading into an oncoming car.

Coincidentally, down towards the end of our street on the same side, Brigitte and Heinz were then leasing a house at 2959 Camino Del Zuro. It was part of another housing tract, but we could see their backyard from ours. Oddly, two streets over Ursula, Earl, Dale and Gale were living on Camino Graciosa. Whendy started Kindergarten here in the neighborhood Weathersfield Elementary School where I often helped as a room mother supervising the finger painting and contributing cup cakes for their parties. Whendy's constant companion at that time was her *imaginary* friend *"Jaime"* with whom she gladly shared her swing set, but when her Dad or uncle Ron went to swing with her she clearly told them with her hands on her hips *"It's not your swing!"*

Dad Earl had parked his twenty foot wooden boat in our side yard where he worked on it every chance he had, proudly scraping, refinishing and repainting it a pretty deep blue color. Dad usually came over unannounced and I would see him out there working happily all alone, relishing the solitude. Those times I brought him coffee and we shared a closeness, just he and I. I cherish the memories.

When this lengthy job was completed we all went to launch his vessel at Lake Casitas. It turned out to be a terrible disappointment especially for Dad, because we only made it a few feet out into the water before the motor broke down. The boat went back on the trailer, but we had a nice picnic before we returned home - I recall Ursula did not participate because my sister Brigitte was present. After that attempted launch he got rid of *"the old tub"* as he called it, and much later it was replaced with his thirty five foot dream boat he called *Earl's Pearl*.

1968 was an unforgettable time in America's history. On April 4, Dr. Martin Luther King was assassinated in Memphis and the following June, Robert Kennedy, the brother of John Kennedy, who had served as

US Attorney General, was assassinated in Los Angeles after he had just won the California primary.

While living on Camino Del Zuro that same year my sister Antje, her husband Walter and two boys Jens and Michael, came from Germany to visit us for five weeks. They stayed with Dave and I for one week and then moved down the street to stay with Brigitte and Heinz. I think it was all a bit strange because we hardly knew one another. Almost eighteen years had passed since we three sisters had been together, and that was when we lived in Berchtesgaden with our mother before they came to take her away to the institution.

I had left Germany as a child and here we were all married with children. However, we had a wonderful time together doing the usual sight seeing: Disneyland, Knotts Berry Farm, Hollywood. We also went on a road trip that took us as far as San Francisco, China Town, Fisherman's Wharf and Monterey where my brother-in-law Ron's parish was at that time. We wound up camping at the base of Yosemite Park in the beautiful *Indian Flat* campground. Antje's boys Jens and Michael buried a silver dollar coin under one of the rocks in the river. They hoped to return some day and maybe find it there still waiting for them. It was an unforgettable visit and by the time they returned home we were the best of friends again.

But I saw less and less of my Mom and Dad. Whendy and Chris were closer to their paternal grandparents and Ruby and Johnny adored our children. We saw them often as they still lived on Montgomery Road and Father Ron came to visit whenever he had the opportunity. He was their rather unorthodox uncle, *the crazy Priest,* setting a fine example when he put on the ugly ceramic mask made by Dave in high school, *"scaring the living daylights"* out of the children, sending them screaming and crying around the house. Or the time he made blaring noises like a police siren telling them the officers were coming to arrest them.

Later we found them both hiding under the bed in Grandma's room. Ron was like a little child himself, laughing so hard his face always turned red and invariably there would be another prank waiting. Whendy and Chris loved every bit of it!

The entire world would remember the end of this decade. In July 1969 Apollo 11 was sent out into space with our astronauts and everyone watched in awe on their television sets as Neil Armstrong actually set foot on the moon.

Dave's obsession during this time was to move somewhere to the *country.* Everyone at that time wanted to *get back to nature* and raise their families in a cleaner environment. Many people were moving to places like Oregon, Montana or Idaho. We had taken a camping trip in our 13' trailer to what would become our favorite retreat, the backcountry of Utah. This is where Dave applied for a job at a radar site and we put the house on Del Zuro up for sale. The house sold, but the job in Utah did not come through. We rented a small house on Calle Clavel and Dave applied for other jobs in other areas, while we waited and he became more restless.

After we sold and left the house on Del Zuro my sister Brigitte sent me a letter in November 1969:

My dear little Barbel!

I don't know how to start this letter, I have an overwhelming feeling stirring within my heart.

This evening as so many other nights I hung some laundry out on the clothesline in our backyard and as always I looked up the street toward your house. But tonight it was all-dark and I realized that you were no longer there. This time it was different than the time you sold your house in Camarillo. It's as though you're already far away from here. Lately every time I see you four I feel a lump rise in my throat.

From the time I first came over from Germany, everything was so much easier for me because you were here my dearest Barbel. I can't imagine what it would be like if you, Dave and the children [whom I love with all my heart] were somewhere far away from us. All I can hope is that you don't journey too far. We may not talk about these things very often but I want to tell you and Dave how much love and understanding, help and fun you have given us.. ".

The jobs, for which Dave had applied, were not materializing and we felt unsettled and decided to buy another home on Sandberg Street in Thousand Oaks.

My memories here are of Chris as a loving little boy who was always running around in his cowboy boots. He literally *"slept with his boots on"*. It was also at this house he had jumped on our bed so high his head hit and broke the ceiling lamp which cut his scalp and put a gash in his leg. We found him hiding quietly, frightened and bleeding under our bed, his huge brown eyes gazing back at me looking like the *Keene* paintings I admired from the 1960's. His eyes really are the windows into his beautiful little soul, still today. The angels have always been with him, especially the day he ran through our 8' sliding glass door.

The most embarrassing moment with him as a three-year-old was in the grocery store when two Catholic nuns, wearing their original black habits, were politely complimenting his big beautiful eyes. It was the time of the "hippie generation" with their often peculiar appearance and wardrobe. Chris' answer to the nuns was a small pointing finger asserting **"Yuk...hippies!"**

Whendy at that time would never have believed that her dreams of having a horse of her own would soon come true.

We set aside some of our capital gains from the sale of our other home and planned a trip to Germany. It was 1970. Whendy was six and Chris almost four. Dave had never been to Europe and it had been fourteen years since I had left to come to America. It was an unforgettable vacation.

We stayed with Antje and Walter, Jens and Michael who lived on Hospital Street #10, next to an old church and ancient graveyard. Walter's wonderful mother, whom we called *Oma* and his aunt had their own apartments in this remarkable old house which had been in their family for hundreds of years. Uncle Walter even had a *"Magic Tree"* for the children, on which small gifts *"magically"* appeared for them every day.

The eight of us traveled through Germany in a VW Van we named *Herbie,* after the Disney movie about a VW beetle. The popular hit song

of the time was *Raindrops keep falling on my Head* and it became our
theme song. We also visited with my oldest brother Dieter who had been a
POW of the Russians from 1944 to 1950 from where he had returned with
some deep emotional scars. The last time I had seen my half brother
Hans-Dieter, who came from my father's 2nd marriage to Anneliese, was
when we were both still children.

We had a fabulous time seeing and visiting all the places Antje and
I remembered as children. The East was still divided and barricaded from
the west by the Berlin Wall. Dave had security clearance but the
Department of Defense would not permit him to cross over into Russian
territory. He had to leave a day to day itinerary at Pt. Mugu in order to be
able to take this trip at all. They were also afraid they might detain me
since I was born in Oranienburg, near Berlin. I know it was quite
enlightening for Dave and he then had more insight into my family
background. He never had a problem with the fact that my father had
been a Nazi and he never questioned me about the photo, which I had kept
secretly hidden away for years.

It was a very sentimental journey that summer, but at that point in
my life I did not yet feel a need to research the past of my father. It is
unfortunate, because at that time there were still many living eyewitnesses
and people who knew of him, who could have given first hand statistics
about my father's involvement at Auschwitz. I was however, not ready to
face that part of my past.

In the meantime Ursula, Earl and Gale moved to Petaluma near
San Francisco. There were no farewells; it was sometime later after their
move that I heard they had moved to northern California.

It was the time of the peace loving flower children that
congregated at the Haight-Ashbury district of San Francisco. Their motto
was *make love not war*, searching for a more free existence, rejecting
materialism. They were a whole new breed of antisocial youths called
hippies, and they were the new culture in the *Age of Aquarius.* Bell
bottom pants, tie-dyed shirts and young people with long hair wearing
headbands united against *the establishment.* 400,000 people flocked to the
"Woodstock" rock music festival in upstate New York. Drugs were used

freely and even Harvard University psychologist Dr. Timothy Leary promoted the hallucinogenic drug LSD.

My little brother Dale was a product of this generation, insisting on wearing his hair long and at age seventeen Mom and Dad could not control his rebellious behavior. When they moved away he stayed behind, living with friends taking odd jobs working as a janitor and at a newspaper, and sometimes attending classes at college. He says he learned more from a couple of black friends who were a great positive influence at that time. But from a young age on he pursued his first love which was music, playing his guitar and singing with various groups of musicians.

Ambitious, but naive and inexperienced in life he "wanted to experience people and life away from home" where he found too many restrictions and control. He has continued to follow his life's dream and has since become an accomplished musician. I didn't see much of him during those years, but my sister Brigitte became his confidant and he would talk with her at length about the things that were troubling him. My sister's home on Calle Damasco was a safe haven for him as well, whenever he felt the need for comfort and security of family.

Eventually, as in my case both Dale and Gale would have to face their own demons, issues that surfaced later in life reverting back to their childhood and the relationships they had with their mother. Today we all have a mutual love and understanding for our Mom, who has been very supportive and loving to all her children.

After Ursula and Earl moved to Petaluma all ties were severed between us and since this was their decision we lost touch with one another. I missed them, but as a result everyday life became easier and a sense of inner peace and freedom came into being during those years. But sometimes I had dreams of Ursula. Often I would awaken with a jolt and felt as though she was calling for me. Later I learned those were the times of either physical problems or times she felt I was calling for her. There was a definite connection and a deep love that has remained even throughout the years of the estrangement between us.

It was a happy time in my life. I loved my husband and my children and for a time it seemed I didn't have a care in the world. I started my own little *Avon* business and built up a nice number of customers. My territory was in the hillsides of the lovely Sunset Hills in Thousand Oaks. It helped to build my confidence and although I actually earned very little I felt like I was at least contributing financially.

In 1972 Brigitte, Heinz and Kye planned to go with us on another trip to Germany. Together we mapped out the entire trip with exciting anticipation. It was to be our family reunion and the first time in years all the Liebehenschel children would be together. This time our children were old enough to remember their adventures. I still see Chris wearing his cowboy boots with his Bavarian *Lederhose* [leather pants] and hat and Whendy in her little blue traditional *Dirndl* dress.

Again we traveled all over Germany also meeting Dave's sister and family in Zweibruecken. My half-brother Hans-Dieter, his wife Anita, who was expecting another child and their two year old son Thorsten, met us somewhere along the Rhine River and also traveled with us. We all went to Austria to see the house in St. Gilgen, which our parents had built during the war. This was the same house from which we were evicted causing us to end up as homeless refugees in 1945.

We all stayed in Berchtesgaden at the Lochner Guest house, the Haus Bergluft where Antje and I had lived as foster children. Our trip ended at my brother Dieter's, where his wife Steffie and two children Gudrun and Michael were awaiting us in Fuerth-Nuremberg for the family reunion. In their back yard under the trees we all vowed emotionally that it would not be the last time we would meet, but in reality it was the last time we would all be together. It was wonderful that we were able to make that memorable journey together.

But when we visited Dachau, a former concentration camp, and saw actual documents bearing my father's signature as part of the exhibits, it was somehow completely incomprehensible, although we all came away feeling a profound emotional impact. It was not yet an issue I could cope with as reality. We only discussed it superficially among ourselves and strangely enough I really believe that my sisters and brothers at that time were in some sort of denial like I was. It was easier to hide it in the farthest corner of our minds.

However, it stirred a very real passionate chord inside of me. A desire for truth awakened within me and after we returned home that summer I started reading *Inside the Third Reich* by Albert Speer. It was only the beginning of a state of mind, which I would some time later call *The Auschwitz Kommandant*.

The next couple years Dave was on an aggressive campaign to obtain a new position elsewhere. He was no longer happy at Pt. Mugu and seemed determined that he needed a change. He was visibly frustrated and it was a time of terrible anxiety for him. Johnny my father-in-law, introduced us to martinis and we often enjoyed one before dinner at night. It helped to calm Dave's apprehension, but of course at that point he had no idea where this path would take him.

Before Christmas in 1973 he was offered a position with [NOA] The National Oceanic and Atmospheric Association, for the National Weather Service in Eureka, on the northern coast of California.

I often wonder, had we known what changes lay ahead of us if we would have accepted this job which was so far removed from the security of home and from the family which had kept us stable and grounded.

Chapter 5. Eureka

By now Dave and I had been married twelve very happy years. On January 4, 1974 with our personal belongings piled into our green station wagon, with the children waiting in the back seat and the 13' camping trailer loaded with all my houseplants, we slowly pulled out of the driveway at Sandberg Street. We were leaving our home in Thousand Oaks to take a job in Eureka, on the coast of northern California. As we headed down our street for the last time our neighbors the Hilden's mother stood at the front window waving good-bye.

We left with conflicting emotions. Dave was taking a job with the Weather Service, unrelated to the type of work he had performed for the Department of Defense at Pt. Mugu, and it would mean a cut in pay. It was also difficult to leave friends and what had been our home since we married in 1962, and for me since I had come from New York. But it was especially sad to leave our family. We were very close to Brigitte and Heinz and Dave's parents Ruby and Johnny. They were all heartbroken about our move.

Since Dave had been tormented with this idea, I wanted it almost as much as he did and always supported him in what he thought was best for us. He was the breadwinner and I respected his good judgment and decisions. I had no idea what to expect, but tried to accept things and do what had to be done. I felt as long as I had my little family around me, that I could handle anything. It was also exciting to think we were starting a whole new life, but it was impossible to hold back the tears as we drove away heading north on the open road. However, as we left Thousand Oaks that day, I had no idea that the happy life I had known until then would soon be lost forever.

We stopped overnight in a motel in the town of Willits and that night all my houseplants within the trailer froze. At that time, Whendy age nine and Chris age six, were most important to us. We stopped to play with them in the snow. Dave was a good father and husband, we were very much in love and very devoted to one another as a family.

After we arrived in Eureka we lived in a rather old, run down motel for a month with no kitchen facility, only a hot plate. It was not in the best section of town. The children went to a neighborhood school temporarily and came home with "*a stomach ache*" every day. It was a definite case of culture shock and they were not happy in their new environment. We knew we had to find a home as soon as possible.

Eureka is an interesting old port city on Humboldt Bay, its' industries consisting primarily of fishing and lumber. The unique Victorian homes are reminders of another era. We were to experience an entirely new and different class of people, which we had never been exposed to in Thousand Oaks. Surrounded by beautiful redwood forests, rivers and streams, we thought we had moved to nature's paradise.

Still, in the motel Dave was very anxious about his new job and a drink after work made circumstances easier for him to cope with. However, I was surprised to see him take a shot in the morning. It was something which seemed to be becoming more apparent and drinking became his daily routine, but more so since our vacations to Germany during the summers of 1970 and 1972. There drinking was casual and a social event enjoyed at anytime of the day.

He worked hard repairing weather service equipment in very remote areas with always the cold and stormy Eureka weather to contend with. One of the most interesting places they serviced was the beautiful old St. George Lighthouse Station near Crescent City, which was still in use at that time. They took a coast guard cutter out near the edge of the rock and from a swinging basket he had to grab hold and *jump* onto the outside railing of the Lighthouse itself. It was not only challenging, but also very dangerous.

Then at the end of their day they were always rewarded with a great sea-food dinner cooked by Mrs. Swanson, the wife of the meteorologist at the St. George Station. She usually sent home delicious jars of fresh homemade Herring and Tuna she had canned herself. It was hard work, but Dave found it very exciting...at first.

There were personality conflicts with Dave's supervisor, and the drinking which had been just to ease things became habitual. Never questioning the reason behind his problems, our physician simply prescribed Quaaludes for his sleepless nights and Valium to calm him during the day. I don't believe that at this point in time Dave realized that he was on a collision course headed for total self-destruction which would eventually end our happy life, as we had known it. Neither one of us had any premonition.

The house we found on Worthington Drive on Humboldt Hill was another great fixer-upper. The view of the ocean and Humboldt Bay was spectacular. The back lot was large enough to hold *Ceta,* Whendy's beautiful Arabian-Quarter Horse and *Pepper,* Chris' Welch Pony. Our neighbor Judy on one side of us owned sheep and llamas, horses and a whole menagerie of ducks, geese and more! Pat and Ed, who lived in a lovely three story split level house on the other side of us, and their children Mike, Dean and Janice became our good friends.

We had many fun Saturday nights out together, dancing to the music of the *NorCal Playboys* at the old Moose Lodge in the midst of the Redwoods. Their big hits were the popular tunes *Behind Closed Doors* and *Easy Lovin'.* Ed was a good dancer and would twirl me around until I was dizzy, having to take many small steps to keep up with his long legs and single strides. Dave and I became even better dancers together.

On the very first Christmas in our house on Worthington Drive we were quickly introduced to the fury of the northern California climate. During a tremendous storm, which uprooted age-old redwood trees, crushing people in their cars, a dedicated UPS man delivered a package to us while we sat in the dark without electricity. In tears, lonely by candle light, I gratefully opened the package sent to us by my friend, Patty. Dave was in a stupor, asleep in his chair and I was lonely and homesick, wondering what I was doing here away from everyone? Dave opened his eyes long enough to incoherently babble about flying *Bubble Gum Trees.* He had more than likely been listening to *Tex Ritter's "Big Rock Candy Mountain"* on his car radio that day. Whendy and Chris thought that was very funny at the time and always covering up, they never had any idea the devastation I actually experienced.

It was more than getting back to nature; it was a whole new life style and a major transition for us. I learned many things in Eureka, and among them was being more independent. I was left alone with the children when Dave was sent to periodic work related schools in Kansas City, sometimes up to seven weeks at a time. I missed him terribly when he was gone and felt like one of the kids myself. He had always been there to take care of me. He was my strength, support and security. I now had to take charge of the bills and ran the children all over the area for their many activities. The responsibilities were good for me, as it was time for me to become less dependent on my husband.

The children and I would be faced with a few calamities the first time Dave was sent to one of his training schools in Kansas City. A skunk somehow found his way into the dryer vent, eventually escaping, but the offensive odor lingered for many days. One night there was a loud commotion coming from the attic. It was frightening, I awoke Whendy [for moral support] and together with a broom for protection I pushed open the ceiling trap door not knowing what to expect. Out sprang a screeching black wild cat that flew past us, climbing up and down our drapes before it finally ran out of the front door, which I had opened. With weak knees I tried not to show my fear and had no choice but to cope with all these unfamiliar situations.

We rented a horse trailer the day we went to pick up *Ceta* out in the country. The children were excited watching as their Dad had hold of the rope to load Whendy's new horse into the trailer. We were definitely inexperienced horse people but learned quickly that day. No one told us that some horses just "don't do" trailers and have to be blindfolded. Ceta reared back and the rope Dave had held ripped off the tips of two of his fingers.

Poor Whendy and Chris turned pale with horror and my knees became jello. Calmly, Dave told me, *"drive me to the hospital!"* Swallowing my fear, feeling my heart beating in my throat, I did. I don't know how but terrified I pulled the empty horse trailer behind us. It was very traumatic for Dave to lose part of his fingers and it would be just another lesson we had to learn. As a result there was more prescribed pain medication and the drinking became worse.

The accident didn't stop us from still purchasing Ceta, however, and she turned out to be a terrific horse for the children. Whendy would proudly tell everyone *"She is the fastest horse on Humboldt Hill!"* Hearing some of the hair-raising tales today it's a good thing the children never told me about all of their adventures and escapades when they rode their horses out in the open countryside and within the property of their favorite "dairy".

Up until now Dave and I had a good loving relationship in our marriage. When he returned home from Kansas City, our love was always renewed as we took time going to the river in the redwoods and playing on the deserted beaches by ourselves.

Gradually, however, more and more he had the physical aura of alcohol about him. His appearance was not what it used to be and I became less important to him. He fell asleep in his chair every night, but not only from physical exertion...and my loneliness began. It was actually frightening because I knew I was losing him.

One of those nights when he was asleep in his chair and after the children had gone to bed I couldn't wake him. I became so frustrated I held his shoulders and shook him furiously, shouting at him *"Why are you doing this to yourself and don't you know what it's doing to us?"*... He never woke up and everything seemed so hopeless I just sat there sobbing. Away from my family and everyone I had known, there was only Pat, my next-door neighbor, who saw much of what was going on. I never discussed my problems and she never said anything, but was silently supportive and a true friend.

Years later she said to me, *"Eddie and I could never understand why you stayed with him!"* My children became my whole world and most important in my life.

However, Dave and I had some good times together those first two years in Eureka when everything we did was new and exciting. As in most logging and fishing communities, drinking is especially prevalent in that area. Although I too enjoyed having good times, I could not and did not care to keep up with him. Dave did try to make up for things by taking me out to some of the wonderful Sea Food Restaurants within the area.

We were hurting financially and a friend who worked at a local Steak House arranged a job for me as a hostess. After a short time I was promoted to waitress. The first night I was on the floor we had a major storm and lost all power. I served three young men by candle light, who were my first and only customers. They left me a large tip, but I realized the Restaurant business was not for me. I did, however, resume my Avon Business.

One February, for my birthday we went to see *Charlie Rich* perform in Reno. We enjoyed his magical show tremendously and it was a wonderful weekend. To our complete surprise, we awoke to snow the next morning and were one of the few people who made it through with our little black VW, before they closed the roads.

Whendy and Chris had been left at home in the care of Kathy, a young woman who was recommended to be a very capable baby-sitter. Shortly after we left for Reno, Kathy supposedly hurt her back and poor Whendy ended up taking care of both Kathy and Chris. After that I never felt comfortable to leave my children with anyone else again.

Whendy and Chris were wonderful children and so very precious to me; they helped fill the void. I was able to give them the love and attention that I had lacked and craved as a young child without my parents, after I was placed in foster care. They would never have to cry for their mother, as I would always be there whenever they needed me.

They were involved in baseball, football and Whendy's track meets were exciting to watch, usually in the cold Eureka fog, all of us wrapped up in blankets. We always brought their friends on outings and picnics along with dogs Shark and Doby. We usually went to our favorite swimming hole at the river, in Meyers flat, nestled among the beautiful redwoods. There was always room to include their very special friend, Janice who was like part of our family. It was a great healthy, outdoors country atmosphere for them in which to grow up.

Yes, we were a close family, but my children knew nothing of my past, about who my father was and about my mother who had been in a mental institution. I believe they did realize that I was adopted, but I intentionally avoided any part of the subject. When my sister and I talked about family matters among us, Whendy sometimes hid nearby, listening to our *secrets* with great curiosity.

We had many friends and family visit us during the summers, and every one of them were in awe of the lovely surroundings we lived in. The exception was Dave's mother when his parents came to visit. She wanted to see the view of the Bay the following morning, but all that was visible were the tips of pine trees enveloped in the thick blanket of fog which usually didn't burn off until later in the day or sometimes not at all. She said, *"I hate this ugly place!"*

Soon thereafter their month's supply of clothing and personal belongings were packed back into their car and they left for a friendlier climate. I can't say we were sorry as at that time we loved everything about the area including the fog and wanted our guests to share our feelings. I even tried to overlook the green mold that grew in our closets due to the dampness. There was always a roaring warm fire burning in our beautiful rock fireplace and our theme song by the Carpenters was *"We've only just Begun to Live."*

We became known for the ideal vacation spot as people knew they would be entertained and treated like family. After two summers of constant company, giving me only enough time in between more scheduled guests, to clean house, wash sheets and cook ahead, I was really becoming tired of all the work. Dave even took time away from work to drive our guests everywhere, as we showed them the many points of interest. Somehow the dream I had of maybe someday owning my own Bed & Breakfast Inn had lost its appeal and no longer seemed as exciting.

Brigitte and Heinz also came to stay with us a few days to celebrate Thanksgiving. Kye had left for the Navy and we missed each other terribly. When they were to return home, after the holiday there was a problem concerning their flight and in order to make connections they needed to get to San Francisco. Heinz called Ursula in Petaluma. She helped them book a flight out and invited them to come stay overnight with them in Petaluma. We left the dinner table as it was - piling the dirty holiday dishes in the sink and packed up in a hurry.

I had severe reservations about going with them, as I had not spoken with Ursula and Earl in quite a few years, not since they had left Thousand Oaks without a word. I had time to think on the way there and wondered if we were doing the right thing? My doubts were soon appeased when we were greeted warmly with a big hug, so like the one I recall Ursula giving me the very first time we met when I was a child in Germany. I fought back the tears.

Their home was a lovely tri-level and they seemed to be doing very well. Dad had been promoted and was now one of the high ranking administrators within the Veterans Administration. He had also earned his teaching credentials and was awarded his degree of *Juris Doctor* by Oklahoma City University. Although it progressed at a gradual pace, our relationship resumed from that day on. But I really dreaded returning home where I would have to face a sink full of dirty dishes.

Soon after our reunion in Petaluma, Ursula and Earl sold their tri-level home and bought a country place in Coos Bay Oregon. The old white house with blue trim on Coaledo Road was on a good sized piece of property. Dad was soon to retire and lived on his boat *Earls Pearl* until that time came. He came home on weekends and Agi, Mom's sister, lived with them for a time. They renovated the house replacing the old foundation and we often went to see them in Coos Bay when we lived in Eureka. Dave even helped Dad when there was a problem with their well. We had little water in the house that weekend, but our children had a wonderful time with their now teenaged Aunt Gale.

We tried to instill good family values and dinnertime around our table was always special. There were no digital devices to distract only family discussions, an important time to bring us together. Often the children invited friends to eat with us; they called us *The Waltons* or compared us to *The Cleaver's* of the old television program *Leave it to Beaver*. Just like *Ward* the father in the TV series, Whendy and Chris believed their own Dad had all the answers and looked to him as the wise important head of our family because he really was. Just as the TV moms, I could always be found in our homey kitchen where I learned how to prepare specialties of the area, like fresh crab and smoked salmon. I felt it was crucial that I was there when the children came home from school, also creating a sense of security for myself as well.

Our camping trips taken in the summers with our 13' trailer were probably the best times we all had together. I loved cooking outdoors over an open campfire when everything always tasted so good. We bathed in the cold creeks or lakes using pure Ivory soap to protect the environment. In the evenings we sat in front of our campfire roasting marshmallows and singing songs. We spent our entire times outdoors and only sat inside when it rained. Those times we played games or colored pictures, like the one I drew of a *"four legged"* duck. Whendy, Chris and their Dad never let me live that one down!

We explored and found many out of the way places, particularly in the State of Utah. There was the slumbering small community of Fremont, where time had stood still. We visited Dave's friend Casey who had a rustic cabin in Fremont with a fabulous garden full of vegetables. He took us out in his canoe and introduced us to *S'mores*. We made many friends like Hyrum and Cora Mae Taylor, but our favorite was the colorful old local character named Merril.

It is a *dry* state and alcoholic beverages had to be acquired through the State Liquor Agency. Our campsite by a little stream became very popular when the locals found out about our wine and hospitality. Especially Merril, who told endless yarns of the good ole' days and of times during the war in Germany when he too was in my adored Berchtesgaden in Bavaria. We even discovered our own *Billy Jack,* a genuine cowboy with lasso and tall black hat. He was the son of *Boot Johnson,* a trail guide and *Wagon Master.* They took us on a hayride down the trail with Boot playing his guitar as we all sang *Home on the Range.* When we reached the top of the butte they built a campfire and we watched the spectacular sunset while we roasted our hot dogs.

Out of nowhere came a strong twister, a small tornado that ripped mercilessly through our campsite. The men held down the wagon while the children and I tried to find shelter. It was really quite eerie and I felt as though we were reliving the times of the pioneers in this *Pine Valley.*

When all was finally calm once again, the kids laughing, gazed at my hand still clutching the hot dog I had been eating which was now covered with dirt and straw. We also went on horseback trail rides.

The most unforgettable landmark of Pine Valley was its' beautiful painted white wooden church built in 1867. This New England-designed church was put together as the ships of early days with wooden pegs and rawhide strips substituted for nails.

Whendy and Chris talked of their childhood and those adventures we shared with great admiration and voiced their appreciation of the togetherness within our family life which few people are fortunate enough to experience. For me those times will always be reminiscent of the happiest during my married life.

I'll always cherish the loving closeness and the memories of Christmas when we made ornaments from dough, into shapes of angels, gingerbread men, snowmen, candy canes and more. We hand painted and decorated them and even their Dad made a Santa Claus signed, *Daddy Dave 1976.* Today they are family heirlooms and every Christmas they recall for me those happy days long ago when our kitchen was cluttered with paints, glitter, excitement and love.

Our first trip to Fern Canyon is particularly memorable. It is a magnificent Canyon right off the beach toward Crescent City on the northern coast. When Heinz and Brigitte visited we brought them there and my sister and I agreed it was a paradise like nothing we had ever seen before. The first time we came across it we had once again traveled in our *"Black Beetle"* along with kids and dog Shark - who by the way had been left by the previous owners of our home on Worthington Drive.

We had to cross a meadow filled with a herd of grazing Elk, and then it was a short hike through woods and over sparkling streams, before we arrived at the actual Canyon itself. What a spectacular sight! The high reaching Canyon walls are covered with a blanket of lush green five-fingered ferns and waterfalls created crystal clear pools below, surrounded by an array of wildflowers. Fallen logs connected the paths making natural bridges over the clear water of *"Home Creek"*. Not many tourists knew of this area and we met very few locals. It seemed untouched by human contamination.

It was late that afternoon and we were on the beach when we tied a magnificent piece of driftwood, which we had found, onto our VW. Dave had already made a beautiful Redwood Burl Top Bar for our family room and this would make a perfect base for a coffee table. Completely unnoticed by us, a storm had closed in and without warning the wind was howling all around us as we were being drenched by the pouring rain.

The driftwood secured to our front bumper was larger than the car itself and when we tried to drive away we only became buried deeper and deeper into the sand. It was getting dark and the beach was totally deserted. It was cold and I couldn't help feeling a sense of panic.

Suddenly in the distance there stood a figure of an old man. It seemed he had come out of nowhere. With my umbrella in hand and seemingly propelled by strong gusts of wind I started running toward him without giving it another thought. The figure before me looked like a painting I'd seen of a sailor with a rough weather-beaten face and a hauntingly fascinating appearance. I said to him, *"We're stuck in the sand and all alone, can you please help us?"* He never said a word to me, but came to help, pulling us out before it became completely dark. We learned later it was *"Crazy Charlie"* a local legend who mysteriously appears and vanishes. Only a chosen few have encountered *Crazy Charlie.* We didn't feel *crazy* was a fair description.

There were many embarrassing and humiliating moments when I tried to *"cover up"* Dave's advancing addiction. Frankly, I wondered how it was possible for him to perform at work because even his speech seemed constantly slurred. Yearning for the man I once knew and loved, I often begged him to stop or even try to slow down the drinking. His mornings began with orange juice laced with gin, but more like gin laced with a little orange juice.

Sitting at our dining table looking down at the Bay, he would squint by closing one eye saying to me, *"I think I must have a tumor because I only see a blur."* It terrified me because the once stable, responsible mate who I could always count on as my best friend, was rapidly disappearing and in his place was a stranger I didn't even know anymore. I was beginning to feel as I had as a child when I was taken from my family, torn from the people I loved and fearful of being left all alone once again. The security and the *sense of belonging,* which were so important to me and that I had always had with Dave was gone.

My life seemed to be out of control. My caring husband and the love of my life stopped loving me. I needed to be loved, but it seemed he was only interested in his bottle. How could this be happening to someone who would force himself to drink a *Baby Oly* [a very small can of Beer] just to be sociable, when I first met him? Yes, I did well at covering up, as people thought we were the perfect couple with a perfect marriage. But we never fooled our next door neighbors and friends Pat and Ed.

Although only psychologically, I started developing seemingly very real physical ailments, brought on by depression and stress. Hyperventilating, I carried a paper bag around with me. There were also heart palpitations, anxiety attacks and I was feeling generally ill. One of these attacks sent me to the emergency room for an EKG, which showed no physical problems.

Whendy's school nurse called me one day, saying, *"I have Whendy in the office, she is very upset and crying. She has seen you breathing into a paper bag and is worried that something is going to happen to you."* So now it was affecting the children! I made a doctor's appointment. He found nothing wrong physically and as he studied my face he wanted to know what was bothering me? I confessed I was having a difficult time coping with my husband's problem. He was very sympathetic and with fatherly compassion said, *"You know, many intelligent, even professional people have tried to come to this area to live, but end up as hopeless alcoholics. Go back to where you came from and if your husband can return to his old job, have him do so as soon as possible!"* It was sound advice and Dave agreed to begin applying for a job back at the Naval Base at Point Mugu.

Our recent trip back to Thousand Oaks the August before also made us realize how much we missed our families and the warmer dryer climate of southern California. That, however, was a sad trip home. We were at Disneyland with Brigitte, Heinz and Dave's parents when Johnny, my father-in-law, had a fatal heart attack. It was at the same time that August that Elvis Presley also passed away. Then even more so we felt the need to return home because Ruby was now all alone at 2112 Montgomery Road..

Chapter 6. Returning Home

Our house in Eureka was placed on the market and early in 1978 Dave received word that there was a position for him on San Nicholas Island. This is where he worked when we first met in 1962. He always had a great reputation, highly respected and liked by his old colleagues who went out of their way to find an opening for him. It was to be temporary until a job came available on the mainland at the base at Pt. Mugu. He accepted the position on the Island leaving me and the children behind to take care of the sale of our home.

He was not sober the morning he pulled away in the little *Black Beetle* and I was terribly worried. Hours later he called from King City, but when I heard the tone of his voice, my heart sank as I knew immediately what sort of condition he was in. He was crying, *"My engine burned up, I don't know what to do!"* Telling me "he didn't know what to do" was something I never thought I would ever hear him say. He was asking *me* for the answers? It was devastating, I felt totally helpless, lost and afraid with a terrible *sinking* feeling, left here all alone with the children. He ended up taking a bus to his brother Ron's parish and after buying Ron's car he then drove on to Thousand Oaks.

He stayed with Brigitte and Heinz on the weekends when he came off the Island. It didn't take long before Brigitte called on a regular basis to inform me of Dave's heavy drinking. They were shocked at his appearance and behavior and I felt sick whenever they called me. They didn't know how to cope with him or what to do to help. I felt completely at my wits' end at that time, horrified that I was no longer there to cover up for him and now the awful truth was being revealed. Before now I don't believe anyone realized the extent of his problem. But now there was nothing more I could do to hide the awful truth. Today I understand that I should not have felt responsible for his actions or even have tried to cover up for him, as by doing this I was what they call an *enabler.* He was the only one who was responsible for him, but he was not ready nor willing to change.

Out of complete frustration, not knowing what to do next, I called him: *"Dave I can't go on like this. If you don't stop drinking I will take the house off the market and stay up here with the children. We can't live together the way things are!"* At this point I felt numb as though our love had died. I no longer knew what my feelings were about him or our relationship. What I did know was that I felt betrayed and abandoned, combined with fear and loneliness. My physical self functioned like a zombie while my heart and mind seemed somewhere outside of my body.

At that moment I even lashed out at Brigitte, furious that she had listened in on our private phone conversation. I didn't need her to interfere in my business, which in all fairness had now really also become her business. I detested his drinking, but still felt loyal and wanted to protect him and not have people say derogatory things about my husband. With both Dave and Brigitte still on the phone I asked, *"Why should I come back? There's nothing for me to come back to!"*

But Dave promised to quit drinking, which was more than he had done in the past - and I agreed to try again. One of the things I disliked most was the fact that now everyone knew our personal business. I had worked so hard to keep things private all those years, even from our closest family. I really was proficient at deception, as I had learned to be throughout my life. How could our lives have come to this?

Our house in Eureka sold and Dave came to pick up the three of us and our dog Doby. Our adopted dog Shark stayed with our neighbor Judy. After we sent the moving van on ahead, we too headed *home* to Thousand Oaks.

Dave had already bought a small house on Calle Nogal only a few minutes from Brigitte and Heinz. It was in the same neighborhood where Ursula and Earl had bought their first home in California on Calle Jazmin. A few blocks away was the apartment on Calle Quebracho which Dave and I had rented as newlyweds. One street over behind us sat the *Country Cousins* market where 16 years earlier I had frantically called Dave from the pay phone about the dent I had put into the side of his car.

Yes, I was happy to be home, but when Dave first showed me through the house he had purchased I fought back the tears and the lump in my throat was choking me. It needed a great deal of work and had little ambiance compared to the lovely home we had left on Humboldt Hill. But then *fixer-uppers* had always been a challenge for us. We would live there for the next ten years.

Eventually we built a whole new master bedroom with fireplace and skylight, also remodeled the entire kitchen. But the first thing we did was put up a large above ground swimming pool surrounded by a wooden deck. It was meant for the children, but we enjoyed it as well. Often Heinz came over on his days off and we all played *marco polo* until evening.

Dave continued working on San Nicholas Island coming home only on weekends, but that would quickly change when we realized Whendy was having problems at school and she needed her Dad's authoritative guidance. I was horrified when the school called me to inquire why Whendy had not attended any of her classes for two weeks. We discovered she had become involved with the wrong crowd and it wasn't only cigarettes they were smoking.

Dave came off the Island to work at the base after that and although he himself was having problems he was always the best father and his presence in our home at that particular time was exactly the guidance his daughter needed. I must admit I felt some guilt that I had not recognized any of the signs. We fortunately caught the trouble before it got out of hand. Shortly thereafter Whendy's life turned around. Heading in a more positive direction, she made new friends and stayed in school.

Chris was of an entirely different nature and as far as he was concerned, smoking or drinking was never an option he would even consider. Around that same time, however, he too was of great concern to us and also had trouble at school. Chris, being the sensitive type, fell victim to a group of bullies at his middle school. Then he contracted mononucleosis and had a difficult time making it through a whole day at school. He invariably would call me on a daily basis at work, pleading with me to pick him up. He was terribly fatigued and didn't have the strength to ride his bike home. I was extremely worried about him and my manager at the Boutique where I was now working was very understanding, letting me leave whenever there was the need.

I would race to the school to pick him up and then get him settled at home on the sofa with drinks, blankets, books, TV etc. I always felt bad having to leave him, but it especially broke my heart when I found his little notes to me that said, *"Thank you Mommie for picking me up. I miss you and love you so much!"* I carried one of those cherished notes with me for years until my wallet was stolen. I was very upset about the loss of my wallet and credit cards, which were all used to their credit line limit by the thieves, but nothing upset me like the loss of that note which was now gone forever.

Reminiscent of my own problems at school years earlier it was important to help him catch up with his studies and we finally arranged for a home teacher. Soon he was able to keep up his grades and slowly recuperate at home. I believed without saying it, he was relieved that the bullies were no longer a threat.

My dreams had long been dashed, lost to reality, and the relationship between Dave and I would never again be what it had once been. After we returned to Thousand Oaks our marriage came close to ending and it would have been a time to separate, but I could not bear the thought of my children growing up within a broken home, with their family torn apart. I didn't want them to experience the loneliness I myself had known as a child. It was then, that I vowed to myself, if I ever left this marriage it would only be after Chris and Whendy were old enough to be on their own.

I still missed the closeness between Dave and I, but for a time we weathered the storm and tried to hold things together. However, there seemed to be an invisible barrier, a permanent separation which Dave brought to my attention especially in our lonely king size bed. Barbara Streisand singing *"The way we were"* on the radio never failed to bring the tears, for I too longed for the way we were. Dave also took up his old habit, justifying that it was *only wine*.

My eyes were opened as to how real his problem still was when we took the children and two of their friends to Disneyland. We were having a good time around the pool of our Hotel when Dave complained of feeling ill. We rushed him to a hospital. The doctor told me he was suffering from excessive alcoholic toxic shock. He warned Dave he had better quit drinking and gave him a vitamin-B injection. His tolerance however was amazing. We told the children that their Dad hurt his back when he jumped into the pool and he slept it off the rest of the day. I was terrified I might have to drive home on the freeway [one of my phobias] and was furious that he would have put us into such a predicament, especially since we were responsible for the safety of other people's children. He recovered enough to drive us back home.

I also realized things would never be the same between us, the night I had to go investigate a burglar alarm that went off at the boutique, which I managed in Westlake. It was midnight when I received a call from our security service. As I dressed and was ready to leave, Dave made no attempt to come along with me. I was stunned; he had always been so protective. He sent me off alone, knowing what dangerous situation I might have to confront. When I arrived at the deserted parking lot twenty minutes later, there was no security there to meet me. I could hear my heart pounding rapidly with fear as I walked alone through the dark corridor, toward the rear entrance. I remember unlocking the door, my hands trembling, not knowing what to expect once I entered. Fortunately it was a false alarm, but I no longer felt safe and protected, and as I drove home I cried for the loss of our love.

I was frequently still experiencing the same anxiety attacks, which had occurred in Eureka. Often things became overwhelming and even one glass of wine or coffee was too strong of a stimulant and I couldn't get any food down. I continued to hide his bottles and pour them down the sink, begging him to stop drinking, but it was all useless.

The next few years were filled with many changes. My Dad Earl came to visit us shortly after our move from Eureka. He slept in Chris' lower bunk bed and I heard his heavy, labored breathing at night. He went to see Dale perform at the Marina where his band was playing and he came home talking with pride of his son the musician. Somehow it was sad because he and my brother had never been close and I believe Earl felt a need to see him perform one last time. He had a wonderful time and I was so happy to have him stay with us.

We had a chance to talk like we used to, but I was shocked when he attempted to tell me that a virus had affected his heart muscle and the only way to save him was to have a heart transplant. I vaguely heard him say the words, there was no sound, and the whole experience seemed to take place in slow motion. I tuned it out and really was half listening. I just couldn't process the spoken words and I never acknowledged what he had said. He wanted to tell me that Mom didn't know he didn't have much time. My God! Why didn't I listen?

Something took hold of me taking me away into another dimension. To think he chose to tell *me,* his oldest adopted daughter, me who he could always talk to. He wanted to tell me about his terminal diagnosis, which he kept hidden from everyone else. I was in complete denial disregarding he ever told me; it was easier to deny it ever happened, I loved him too much! I hope he understood my peculiar behavior. I recall something interesting he said to Whendy at that time, *"Don't let your social life get the best of you!"* He died a few months later on June 5, 1979. Strangely enough my own Papa, Arthur Liebehenschel, had the same rare heart disease caused by a virus.

The next few years Brigitte and I became even closer. We took a modern dance class at the high school together recalling the time long ago when we were ballet students of Eva Weigand in Germany. Although this was hardly a comparison and definitely far from disciplined, when we managed to get ourselves entangled during the *dance of the scarves.* We caused quite a disturbance laughing throughout the entire session, with the instructor observing us in total disbelief.

In 1981 Whendy entered the *Miss Thousand Oaks Beauty Pageant* bringing back memories of twenty years earlier when the lions at *Jungleland* roared at me on stage. *Jungleland,* however, was long gone and although Whendy didn't win she was by far the most beautiful.

1981 was also a grim time when my sister Brigitte was diagnosed with Breast Cancer and had to undergo a radical mastectomy. After a year of chemotherapy and radiation treatments they told her the cancer was in remission. It was a difficult time for the whole family.

That following summer we all - including the kids' friends Scott and Cathy - went on another trip to Utah in a rented motor home - hoping it would be inspirational and encouraging for Brigitte. We showed them around all of our favorite haunts and even went on another hayride with our old friend the wagon master *Boot Johnson*. I still hear Heinz singing *On the Road Again* while driving our large motor home. It was fun, but somehow our lives would never be the same.

My sister wrote to me:

"Just a little note to thank you for the cake and all the nice things you do for me. I know it has not been easy for you and sometimes you don't know what to say...just like me. I would like so much to hug you and cry my heart out, but I don't because it would make you feel sad....so I don't show my real feelings. I love you so much." Brigitte 1982

Often Brigitte called me at work and I knew she wanted so badly to talk to me and express her fears, but I would never give her the chance to let her talk about her illness. When I look back, I am so sorry and wish I had let her express the things that were on her mind. But I was selfish because I just could not handle the pain. Denial was easier, although the truth was undeniable.

Life however did continue. Whendy graduated from Thousand Oaks High in 1982 followed by Chris in 1984. It made me especially proud but somehow a nagging sadness reminded me of Baldwinsville, New York twenty years earlier. Ruby who had been living in a retirement home in Thousand Oaks passed away in June 1984.

The year we returned from Eureka I had started working part time in a fashion boutique in Thousand Oaks at the original *Janss Mall* and ended up managing their new shop in the up-scale-neighboring Westlake Village. The added responsibility of running the boutique made my life easier to cope with. I had already single-handedly managed and done the buying for *B&I Fashions* before the owners offered me the position in Westlake. I loved my job, but could not identify with people who lived solely in a material world, as for me money is not the only indication of being successful. Many celebrities shopped in our store and it was here that I met Mickey Rooney. He saw me alone through the window one day and came in to tell me with great charisma *"You have a lovely store!"*

Our sister Antje visited several times. She had remarried, but unfortunately this was not a happy marriage and she came alone with her small son, Pierre. Brigitte had lived with the ongoing guilt of having left Antje alone with our ill mother on that day long ago when she took only me away with her. Her entire life Brigitte had felt responsible for the terrible neglect Antje had suffered with our mother. Of course she wasn't to blame, but the plane tickets given to Antje for her visits to Thousand Oaks made her feel she could show her love and somehow make it up to her.

We had wonderful times taking them to all the amusement parks, to a cabin at Big Bear and days at the Beach house at Sea Cliff which was owned by Heinz' employer. Antje's last visit to Thousand Oaks was during the summer of the 1984 Olympics in Los Angeles.

Dave and I still wore the facade of the happily devoted married couple. Sometimes I think we even had ourselves convinced. On our 20th Anniversary we went back to Yosemite and for our 24th Dave surprised me when a limousine picked me up at work, brought me home, waited so I could change and then proceeded to take us to the *Sand Castle* a lovely restaurant on the Beach at Malibu. It was wonderful, but nothing had really changed, only the ever-widening distance between us.

We also vacationed in various Bed and Breakfast Inns, visiting places like the wonderful ghost town of *Bodie* near the Nevada State border, Napa Valley and all the great wineries, Clint Eastwood's Hog Breath Inn in Carmel, Grand Canyon and the lovely quaint little artist colony of Cambria.

I always had a good time, but sharing these moments with the husband who was so distant was almost worse than being there alone. It hurt so deeply, but I also felt he still loved me although I often wondered what he was really feeling. Was he just pretending that all was well? Even my sexiest red negligee and hi-heels were not enough to spark the love we once shared which I now assumed must have died. I began to believe there was something terribly wrong with me.

Evenings after I came home from work, I prepared dinner, cleaned up the kitchen and then retreated to our lovely new bedroom in order to avoid the verbal abuse brought on by his drinking, which he could never remember the following morning. At those times he sarcastically called me *"Little Miss Perfect"* and I learned it was impossible to reason with an alcoholic. I was unable to penetrate the boundary that had divided us.

In 1987 my Mom Ursula married Jesse. They lived near Sacramento and later moved to Las Vegas.

One Saturday when I came home after work, Dave was in a panic about the new neighbors who had put up some chicken coops and how the general condition of the neighborhood was deteriorating in value. He said, *"Let's sell the house and invest the money into a home for our retirement. I'll take an early retirement from the Government and in the meantime we'll look around for a place and location where we can spend our retirement years."* I became even more depressed. Dave was only six years older than I was, but at forty-five I had never felt my age. I wasn't ready to sit on a front porch watching life pass me by.

Our house was listed with a Real Estate Agency and a *caravan* of multiple Realtors came to view our home. One of the Realtors who came with the group was *Darren – [alias]*. He was a tall, good looking, younger man and I found myself very attracted to him. He flirted and teased and made me smile. He aroused feelings in me that I had forgotten existed, but I was ashamed for feeling this way. He asked me *"How much older is your husband?"* Dave's drinking had aged him considerably at that time and some people thought he was my father.

The house sold and we leased a very nice two-story town house, with a great loft in Newbury Park only a few miles away. Chris moved with us into the private suite located on the ground floor. Whendy was already sharing an apartment with friends. Our accountant informed us that the gains from the sale of our house had to be reinvested into another residence within a two year time period in order to avoid paying a capital gains tax. So now we were forced to look for another home immediately and reinvest our profits or stand to lose a great deal.

We began looking outside of our area where the homes might be more affordable. I remember we looked into a Mobile home park in Paso Robles where I saw an old lady wearing a bathrobe shuffling slowly down her driveway with big furry house slippers. I burst out into tears and told Dave, *"I'm not ready for this!"*

Our Realtor put us in touch with an agent in Santa Maria to show us some properties there. Dave was far from sober the weekend we went to Santa Maria. To my complete surprise and horror, he made very obvious brazen advances toward the woman who was our agent. I was actually shocked to think he was behaving that way right in front of me and mortified as it was very humiliating, but I believe the woman was more embarrassed for me than herself. This disgusting display of seduction toward another woman was a side of my husband I had never known. We had always been devoted and true to one another and I had always felt I was *the only one* in his life. Besides being deeply hurt I was confused and angry.

Darren called me one day and I surprised even myself when I said to him, *"Why don't you come by to see our Townhouse?"* I was excited at the thought and completely astonished, but then afraid when he answered, *"All right I'll see you this afternoon, I'm showing a house in that area."* Had I lost my mind? Did I know what I was doing? But I really didn't need to make excuses to myself because of course I knew.

At that point in time of our relationship I must honestly admit that I really didn't care about what the consequences could be. Darren came and after I showed him around we sat on our patio and talked for a long time. As he went to leave our eyes met seductively and he must have sensed how lonely I was. He took me into his arms and kissed me gently. *"Is this what I'm supposed to do?"* he asked. It had been so long that I had forgotten how wonderful it felt to be held so close by a man. I told myself it was wrong, but after he left I couldn't stop thinking about him. Maybe there was nothing wrong with me after all?

I was swept up by longings I couldn't control and desperately yearned to be loved and held and told I was still pretty and desirable. Looking back today, I realize how terribly unhappy I really was to act as I did, which was so completely out of character for me. The distressing circumstances in my life had driven me to the edge of hopelessness.

Not only was my marriage falling apart, but Brigitte's illness also reappeared in a more advanced stage and my younger half brother, Hans-Dieter in Germany was also dying of cancer. This was a time I had really needed the love and understanding from my husband and best friend, but I felt all-alone. Perhaps he did too?

October was our wedding anniversary and usually Dave and I went on a trip somewhere. This year his drinking was worse than ever and it led me to suggest that he might seek some help from his brother Ron at his parish. I told Dave I was really too afraid to drive anywhere with him in his condition. Once again I pleaded with him, *"You have to do something if you care at all about our relationship. I'm afraid of what might happen I don't understand my feelings anymore. Please get some help!"* As I hugged him I wanted to tell him he was driving me into the arms of another man and I wondered if he still loved me? He left for his brother's and I was optimistic.

Darren was a short-lived temptation. I saw him on one other occasion when he listened with empathy about my sister Brigitte, who was once again in the hospital. Darren walked away that day and I went to visit Brigitte at Los Robles Hospital, feeling guilty and totally disillusioned. I felt that I had finally hit rock bottom, drawn into a deep dark abyss from which there seemed no escape. I was filled with confusion and anguish, a time in my life where it could have been much easier to give up, but I left for the hospital because my sister needed me... and what about my children?

As I drove to the hospital, my mind in a dim fog I thought *"Oh my God, is this really happening to me...to my family?* I asked for the courage and strength to go on.

Brigitte looked so small hooked up to the IV's and monitors, but she was happy to see me and we made idle conversation. I was surprised when she asked me, *"Do you still love Davey Boy?"* He had been to see her, she told me, and he had been crying, but since she had lost much of her hearing she couldn't understand everything he had said to her. I answered, *"Sometimes!"* then laughed it off and told her, *"Don't worry, everything is fine, he's just been drinking a little too much lately!"* She was talking, but it was I, this time, who didn't hear a thing she was saying. Of course things were far from fine, but I tried to keep my personal problems to myself, even from my closest family.

I could never let down my guard even when the burden became too much to bear. I felt numb and relieved to get back outdoors into the fresh air and warm sunshine to help clear my mind.

The young man in the wheel chair whom I had come to know on this floor of the hospital, greeted me with his usual smile. He walked with me down the dismal corridor that had the repulsive smell of sickness, but that day it was more of darkness and death. He wondered why I was in such a hurry today? It was all so heartbreaking and so unfair, this courageous man in a wheel chair, and having to watch helplessly while my sister was bound to her bed, her bones now so brittle and frail she broke one of her legs just by standing up on them. Again I cried all the way home, trying to focus through a blur of hot stinging tears.

When I arrived home I received a phone call from my brother-in-law, Ron. There had always been a special brotherly bond and understanding between Ron and me. When we had first returned from Eureka in the midst of our personal turmoil, Ron was experiencing his own dilemma. Uncertain about his path in life, Ron lived with us for a time when he was on a year's leave of absence from the priesthood. We had each other to talk to when Dave was out on the Island during the week and he told me stories and we joked about his adventurous job at *The Beanery.* He actually worked at a fast food restaurant before he was hired by the *Jerry Lewis Muscular Dystrophy Foundation*, working for the *Jerry Lewis Telethon.* He quickly became disillusioned with life on the outside and realized he could never be anything but a Catholic Priest.

During our phone conversation he said, *"How long is Dave intending on staying here? I don't know what to do with him!"* I really didn't understand this conversation. I thought the purpose for the visit was for Ron to help Dave with his problem? I asked if Dave was still drinking. *"Yes he is,"* was his answer. I had dealt with this problem for well over ten years and when Dave finally reached out to his family for help, three days seemed to be all that could be tolerated. I genuinely felt sorry for Dave. Ron went on to say, *"I should warn you Bobbie, he's really throwing the money around. Today at a restaurant he was coming-on to the waitress, even taking pictures of her with his camera. He left her a substantial tip. Just thought you should know."*

I felt sick and found myself trembling, but all I could say was, *"Oh..thank you for telling me."*

Realizing Dave was not trying to help himself, I told Ron, *"Maybe he should just come back home."* Ron thought that was a good idea. As I hung up the phone the doorbell rang. It was Whendy. She wondered why I was upset and without going into detail I told her that her Dad and I were having some problems. I don't believe she realized how serious they were.

Ron called back the following day after Dave had left him. He was worried because he saw bottles in the trunk of his car. I promised I would call him the moment Dave arrived home and couldn't help but feel sorry for Ron too. He was more than qualified when it came to counseling people within his own parish. I also understood how difficult it was to help someone who didn't want to change or even try to help himself, especially someone close to you. It was a very powerless feeling.

I kept thinking of what Ron had told me about the waitress and had a feeling Dave would stop for a drink at the little neighborhood *Pub* before coming home. It was just up the street from our townhouse. He had taken me there for dinner and I realized then that he had stopped there on other occasions. I was convinced he would stop there before returning home and had the idea to surprise him by meeting him there.

I dressed, fixed my hair and found myself excited at the thought he was coming home. I sat in a booth and so I wouldn't look conspicuous I ordered a *split* of Champaign, waiting...secretly hoping when he saw me he would find me as desirable as the waitress he had taken pictures of. I wasn't used to being in a bar by myself and felt very uncomfortable. As I looked around me, the back of the man at the bar looked familiar. I walked over, holding my breath and then was extremely relieved that it was who I had suspected, an old acquaintance. He was surprised to see me, *"What are YOU doing here?"* he wanted to know. I explained I was waiting here to surprise my husband, whom I thought should be here soon.

He came and sat by me in the booth and I felt less like a *barfly.* I had known him, not too well, for about ten years and we became engaged in a pleasant conversation. He was very handsome with thick wavy hair and a mustache and I tried to ignore those familiar feelings of desire.

Dave did not show up and we left the Pub together, continuing our conversation on a nearby park bench only minutes away. He said, *"Do you remember the times I stopped by the shop in Westlake? I came to see you not because I happened to be in the neighborhood."* I had actually wondered about those times he came to say *"hi"* for no apparent reason, especially when he never seemed interested in talking about his own family. He then said in a whisper, *"You are so very sexy I couldn't get you out of my mind."* It was thrilling and I wanted to hear more. He drew me close to him and kissed my lips passionately. *"You are a good kisser"* he told me.

When his hand brushed against my leg he surely must have felt the garter on my thigh. I had worn a sexy little chemise with garters and stockings under my red sweater and black silk pants, worn to welcome home my husband. So what on earth was I doing in this park with *HIM?* I didn't want to leave, but pulled away saying, *"I really have to get home!"* He wanted my phone number; I gave it to him.

When I arrived home, no one was there, but it was not long before Dave pulled up. We hugged and he said he had missed me. Tears burned my eyes and I had an overwhelming feeling of incredible loss. There will always be feelings of love and compassion for him, for the person he once was, for the memories of a lifetime we had shared together. Tearfully he sat on the edge of our bed quietly mumbling under his breath, *"You'll always be able to find someone else, but I wouldn't know how if I wanted to."* Did that mean that he wanted to? I wondered about the waitress, but didn't mention it, and what about my own questionable actions? Didn't these kinds of things only happen to other people? It was surreal that our lives had become so messed up. It was as though at that instant we both knew it was over and from the very bottom of my soul surged an unbelievable heartfelt sorrow.

"He" called that night, I picked up the phone next to Dave's chair where he sat having his drink and feeling no pain. *"Did he get home?"* I answered *"Yes"*. *"Why don't you meet me somewhere tonight?"* *"Oh no, I can't, but I'll call you tomorrow."* After I hung up I told Dave, *"That was Joyce, she wanted me to meet with the girls tonight."* He was befuddled, but I could hardly believe what I was saying. It was the sort of game of deceit I had never played before or ever wanted to, something I never would have dreamed of doing, something that I despised and could not tolerate in other people. Oh what a tangled web we weave! I didn't like it and I knew the end result was a losing game for which there were never any winners.

"He" called me several times and I would meet him in the park, but it was never a comfortable situation. He talked about his family and I about Brigitte and the whole agony of what was happening in my life.

It seems he was searching for something and I had needed someone, but I also felt it was not the first time for him and this was not the direction I wanted to take. I suppose for the moment I was only reaching out to someone who would listen to me and those few stolen moments of compassion brought me some peace of mind. Neither of us gave in to anything more than an innocent flirtation, as I realized this was not the answer to my problems, because in the end I would have to take responsibility and face the circumstances alone.

Although they were innocent rendezvous, I can't say that I thought it was morally right or in the least bit honest. But I also never felt I was being unfaithful, as the vow *Till death do us part* referred to a relationship which had actually died long before - when Dave chose the bottle over his love for me. I had been very happy for many years and it was never my intention to go out to look for some new adventure.

At that time, however, beside my loneliness was my concern about my sister Brigitte, whose health was becoming progressively worse. She had been in and out of the hospital numerous times. I went to visit her everyday, making friends and sharing the pain and grief of terminal illness with the other families on the third floor, known as the Oncology section of Los Robles Regional Medical Center.

Brigitte was sent home once again before Thanksgiving in November of 1988. Christmas, our favorite holiday, would be met with incredible difficulty, unlike the previous years together, as her prognosis was not hopeful.

Lims Fashions, for whom I had worked for the past ten years, closed their Westlake store adding to the trauma of what was left of my life at that time. I went job hunting, but my heart was not in it and I could not focus and I then decided that it was more important to spend as much time as possible with Brigitte and to be supportive to her husband Heinz. Their only son Kye, who had married Kriste in 1979, and who now had a little boy named Nicholas had his own sorrow to contend with.

Heinz would leave the front door unlocked for me at their home on 2850 Calle Damasco, where they had lived for the last twenty years and where our families had experienced so many happy times together. Their dogs greeted me everyday when I arrived and their loud bark would signal Brigitte that I had come, since she had lost most of her hearing due to the illness. I could always tell my visits were the highlight of her day when I came into her room and she lit up with a loving smile.

The last year of Brigitte's life passed before me like a bad dream. Walking with a cane and unable to hear most of what was going on around her, she was able to attend Whendy and Drake's wedding on February 20, 1988. She was there to take part in her godchild's important day, the little girl she always wished she could have had. She should have had more children; she loved and spoiled mine. Chris often stayed overnight at their house and he and his Aunt Brigitte read or watched *scary* movies. She would spoil him with all kinds of treats and he never left before she forced a few dollars into his pockets.

Beside my personal dilemma my whole life at that time centered around my sister who was fading rapidly. Now the tables were reversed and I looked out for her welfare and tried to make what time she had left as joyous as possible. In the past she had been a mother figure for me, even when she was still a child herself. How fortunate for me that she had made the move to America, giving both of us the opportunity to be best friends and to once again have her be a part of my life.

This day with her I prepared cabbage rolls for their dinner and she was happy that I was scurrying about her kitchen, knowing how I enjoyed cooking. Since she couldn't hear me I communicated by writing her notes on a pad. As time went on she even had trouble focusing on these words on the paper. *"Do you think you'll be able to come over to our house for Christmas Dinner?"* I wrote. She answered, *"Yes, I'd really like to see your new townhouse. It's a two-story isn't it? But I don't think I'll be able to make it up the stairs."* I reassured her, *"I can make you a bed downstairs on the living room sofa or wherever you would be comfortable."* I sat by her side next to the hospital bed that Heinz had rented. Often we held hands. It was so difficult, but I pretended all was well in a listless state of denial. Neither one of us was ever able to face what was the agonizing truth of her prognosis. It was only those times when no words were spoken between us and our eyes met in excruciating silence, that we were unable to disguise what our tormented hearts already knew. Outside her window she could faintly hear the noise of a loud motor. I wrote on the pad, *"Poor Heinz has his work cut out for him with all those leaves blowing around."*

She had ordered all her Christmas gifts through the catalog this year and showed her excitement as I helped her open the boxes delivered by UPS. I wrote, *"I'll wrap everything for you, it'll be fun."* One box held a beautiful gold Angel. She seemed so pleased and smiling told me, *"This one belongs to you!"* I wrote, *"You shouldn't have told me, I would never have known, but it's beautiful and I love it!"* Still smiling she said, *"It's even more beautiful than I expected!"* All three of us sisters have always had a great love for angels and candles long before it became a new age craze.

We talked of Christmases past and agreed that the memories we shared of our childhood and those times we received few gifts when we were poor were most precious. Wonderful of course were those years we were able to spend together in Thousand Oaks watching our families grow. She recalled Christmases with our father who I never knew. She told me of the Christmas trees she remembered during her childhood in Germany, long before I was even born and how our father strung the tinsel so carefully on each branch. I could only remember one particular Christmas with our mother. It was when we lived in Berchtesgaden in two small rooms and my most cherished gift was the *Struwelpeter* book. This Christmas with my sister was to be the saddest of my entire life.

She slept more frequently and I would leave her with a note on the nightstand next to her bed. *"You were sleeping so soundly, so I left at 2:00pm. I peeled some potatoes for Heinz. When you wake please take your pills. I'll see you tomorrow. Love you lots.. Your Baby Sister P.S. It was fun opening the boxes. XO XO XO....."*

Even though I never really wanted to leave her during those days and felt the urgency to seize every moment I still had with her, I found myself almost running out to my car to escape. I needed to get away, as the house was closing in on me. The therapist who came every day told me to do something for myself to clear *the cobwebs, which* were obviously suffocating me. Physically and emotionally it was as though all life was being pulled out of me as well. I wondered, was there even the slightest possibility that everything could turn around and we could all be a happy family again? What was happening to my life? Everything was crumbling around me and there was that constant sick feeling in the pit of my stomach to remind me it was not a bad dream. Nothing seemed real, however, and I felt so alone.

Soon it was becoming more difficult to communicate with Brigitte as she had lapsed into a semi-coma not recognizing who we were. One day she surprised all of us when she sat up straight in bed, looking at the home care nurse, and pointing at me she said, *"That's my sister Barbara!"*

her expression radiated with sisterly love. It was probably one of the last lucid things she said to me or anyone.

Christmas 1988, our otherwise happiest time of the year, came with overwhelming sadness without hopes or dreams to ring in a New Year. Dave and I and our children were there with Brigitte and Heinz, Kye, Kriste and Nicholas. Tearfully we opened the gifts that Brigitte had ordered with so much love and excitement, which I had wrapped mournfully and then placed under their tree that we all had helped to decorate this year. It was a task that had been a special pleasure for Brigitte every year in the past.

December 28th was Brigitte's 56th birthday. Antje called her from Germany and I held the phone up to her ear. Antje attempted to sound cheerful and I fought back the tears. Once or twice Brigitte actually opened her eyes and nodded in acknowledgment to the voice of her sister coming from the other end of the receiver. It was their last communication.

On the afternoon of December 30th 1988, I left her sleeping and kissed her good-bye about 3:00pm. Heinz called at 9:30pm that evening to tell us Brigitte was gone. It was a relief to know she was no longer suffering, but although we knew it was inevitable, we were all in a state of shock. Half an hour later I kissed her cold body for the last time. She now had a peaceful appearance of a much younger woman, that expression of pain and stress, which had distorted her face for so long, had taken leave.

I wondered if her spirit would remain with me? After they took her body away there was a sterile emptiness in her room and in the entire house where I had spent so many wonderful times with my sister. I didn't want to leave. I wanted to experience that last lingering feeling of her presence. Loss is something we all have to face eventually, but I felt the grief well up inside of me. Completely exhausted from all the previous months, I wanted to cry out, *"Oh my God, death is so final. How will I ever be able to live without her?"*

The house on Calle Damasco suddenly seemed shrouded in a dark gray haze, which would never quite lift or vanish. Our once happy, sheltered days within those walls, full of fun, sunshine and hope would never return. No more would I experience the warmth and closeness of special holidays or my sister's wonderful cozy family dinners, which had brought us all together in the past.

We left Heinz alone with Kye, as there were no words that could bring comfort that night. It was the end of an era and for me the final episode to end this phase of my life, leaving me with a lonely void that would never be filled.

The last time *"He"* called me was the day we had just returned from Brigitte's burial at sea. We had waited almost two weeks for the storms to pass for calmer seas and safer boating conditions. It was a beautiful crisp day in January as I stood on the deck of the boat - chartered through the *Neptune Society* - which would take Brigitte's ashes to their final destination. The Pacific Ocean reflected many shades of blue and a cold exhilarating wind pierced through me. The shoreline vanished and reappeared in repetitious intervals while the relentless waves tossed the boat up and down. I was acutely aware of the sea gulls that had followed us and I heeded their haunting call while replaying the images, which depicted a whole lifetime, shared with this sister. It reminded me of that other time, thirty two years earlier when a ship took me away from my sister, but this time another vessel was taking her away from me once more. In the confines of our own minds each of us was now left with only our personal memories.

I remembered her as the pretty youthful sixteen year old girl, with shining black hair, pirouetting across the dance floor at the Eva Weigand Ballet School, who had courageously rescued me when I was a starving child. I recalled that night long ago in Germany when she gave me the photo of my father. I didn't know it then, but it would become the motive, which would later change my life's direction forever.

As the early afternoon sun glistened off the water, Heinz and Kye cast Brigitte's ashes along with fragrant flower petals, into the sea. Paralyzed I watched the trail they left before they were carried away by the waves. My thoughts returned to happier times when we played on the beach at Sea Cliff not far from here, sipping Champaign with strawberries while we watched the sun slowly sink beneath the horizon. A part of me died along with her that day. I miss her terribly. Still today I often long to pick up the phone to hear her say *"Hi Spatzl!"*

Now my life style and routine would have to change drastically. That was a frightening realization for me. No longer could I hide in the shadows, feeling safe and secure behind my sister's imperative need for me. I now had to face what was left of my own life. I wasn't really sure of who I was...but was I ever? I had lost the responsibility of my job, our home had been sold and with it the foundation and stability that had once grounded our family. My children were grown and now Brigitte was gone and what about my marriage? I would have to take control and focus on what lay ahead. It would become one of the most difficult transitions in my life.

I didn't know how or where, but I wanted to make a new start and go on - somehow I eventually did. Somewhere in the back of my mind lingered the thought of what Brigitte had so often expressed and maybe I could even write a book about my father and our family...?

Chapter 7. The Final Chapter

After looking into other surrounding areas to see what the housing market had to offer, Dave and I found a beautiful home in Palmdale. It was a two story dream house and we watched it being built, going there every weekend to see it in its' various building stages. On August 12, 1989 we moved into our Riviera Court home on the desert. It was the last attempt and final turning point of our life together.

I didn't like leaving the children and our town that had been home for so long, but somehow nothing seemed to matter much anymore and maybe the new surroundings would help. I had cleaned the townhouse in Newbury Park leaving it spotless as I had done with every home we had ever left or sold. I called to say good-bye to Heinz and cried when I heard his familiar strong voice. He said, *"Little one, take care of yourself!"* He was like my brother and the shared grief over the loss of Brigitte had brought us even closer. I didn't know then that I would never see him again after leaving that day. We later talked on the telephone, but only for birthdays and holidays or things concerning Dave.

Dave was still working at Pt. Mugu living with Heinz, coming home to Palmdale only on weekends. I started to work at another Boutique and it helped pass the time. I kept busy getting the house and myself into shape, signing up at a tanning salon and gradually lightening my dark hair. Brigitte was gone and now the black hair was only a sad reminder. My inner self continued to grieve. However, I enjoyed the new discoveries of desert living. We had a wonderful view of the desert Joshua trees, which grew in the open landscape surrounding our tract of homes. I pulled myself together to reach a better state of mind, but with Brigitte always there just a thought away.

Still nothing had changed. Heinz would call to tell me of Dave's constant drinking and that he even carried the bottles wrapped in brown paper bags in the trunk of his car. He was worried about him and felt his health was failing. I cooked and froze extra amounts of food on the weekends and packed him plates of ready food for him to eat during the week so he would have some nourishing meals. I looked forward to him coming home on the weekends and prepared the house and cooked his special favorites.

This was to be a whole new beginning for us, but on the weekends, as he sat in front of the TV with his wine I wondered what sort of future we could ever have together? After almost 15 years of this, my feelings at that point had been dampened.

On Sunday October 1, I had to work, but afterward he was going to take me out to dinner. I said, *"Let's do something different and go to that "Edelweiss" German Restaurant."* He agreed. I didn't know that dinner at this restaurant on this very night was going to be the beginning of a major abrupt change toward that future I was wondering about.

Dave told me to reserve a table while he parked the car. I walked through the entrance and there directly facing me sat a very good looking man. Our eyes met, sending a shock through me and I sensed this was trouble. His hair was very blonde, his eyes blue and I had a de-ja-vu feeling that I had known him before.

Dave and I stood just inside the door waiting for a table. The man sat facing me and we couldn't take our eyes off one another. Dave and I were finally seated in the back room. I sat facing toward the back with Dave opposite me across the table looking to the front of the restaurant.

A few moments later the blonde man was seated at a small table facing me. He was very tall and his head almost touched the low ceiling. I somehow sensed an aura of a sad loneliness about him. I don't believe our meeting was just a coincidence. It was much more than a physical attraction. There was a shared sense of spiritual magnetism and energy that seemed to be *pulling* us together. It was a magical fantasy all said with our eyes, which I've only seen happen in the movies. The most exciting encounter of my life and I doubted it could ever happen again.

Dave was absorbed in the wine and unaware of the *electricity* around us, while I wished the night would never end. When our bill came the waitress asked for our telephone number on the charge slip. Dave kept repeating, slurring the words, *"my number is....."* loud enough for everyone in the restaurant to hear it. I really hated to leave that night and wondered if I would ever see this stranger again.

A few days later I received a call at home and a very sensual voice said, *"Hi, do you know who this is?"* I was astonished, but had an idea and asked, *"How did you get my number?"* [Of course I knew how and was surprised more people that were at the restaurant that evening hadn't called!] We talked it seemed for hours and the next time he called we set up a meeting in a very *incognito* place.

But the night we met, I found the *inconspicuous place* packed with a room full of people watching the big screen for Monday night football. I located a single empty table, crowded among loud fans and I waited nervously. I saw him coming. He was wearing a red corduroy shirt and then he bent down to kiss me on the cheek. I was a little afraid, but still filled with excitement. We found a more quiet corner off by ourselves and he ordered us a bottle of Champaign. His name was John. (alias) We talked until closing time. I thought I must be losing my mind.

He told me that something beyond his control had drawn him back to the restaurant the night of October 1, telling him to *"get back to the Edelweiss now!"*. He had been in there earlier for a glass of dark German beer, but it seemed he could get no one to serve him. When he saw me walk in, he recalled thinking to himself, *"God she's beautiful, but is that her father or her husband?"* He asked for a table off in a corner where he could be by himself, and as though it was planned, he was seated where we were almost forced to gaze at each other.

After Dave and I left that night, John took my pink napkin from our table wondering if I had left him some sort of message inside. He stayed until closing time hoping I might come back by myself. He says it was a *Fairy Tale* planned by a higher force.

We saw each other frequently after that and it was a very exciting time in my life. John was so different, not predictable as life had always been with Dave. Everything was a new adventure and we did things on the spur of the moment. He made me happy and I found myself smiling again. He was a very spiritual person, interesting to talk to and I had someone to share my loss of Brigitte. We found we were truly soul mates. I heard some of the women at my work whisper, *"She must be meeting someone after work, she's always redoing her make-up and hair before she leaves for home."* They knew my husband was gone during the week. I could actually feel myself *glow* and had no thoughts of hiding these incredible feelings. I felt so alive, on a constant natural cloud of euphoria and I thought I was in love...how could this be wrong?

When John and I met it had also been a low point in his life and my first impression of loneliness about him was true. He told me, *"I felt that day that my whole world had come to an end and there was nothing left for me."* We seemed to be good for each other at that point.

Sometimes I stayed at his house in Lake Elizabeth and he cooked for me. How wonderful that was! I would drive home in the early hours of the morning and often strangely sensed someone was following me. Many times we met someplace and parked my car taking his car and later in the evening retrieving mine where I had left it parked earlier. A few times I found a note on my windshield that said *"Hi!"* It looked like familiar handwriting, but how could that be? I didn't know what to think. Dave had even discouraged me to call him at work at Pt. Mugu, which frankly puzzled me and when I did call him he wasn't there.

Very strange happenings were occurring! I heard static on my phone line. One weekend Dave told me of a supposed *dream* he had of me driving on a country road. I realized he was describing the winding road to John's house in every detail. It was becoming too bizarre and also a little frightening. What was going on? He knew things that could only have been known if someone was listening in on my phone conversations or had been stalking and following me.

On Thanksgiving Day that year Dave confronted me asking if I was seeing someone else. I felt I owed him the truth and admitted, *"Yes I am."* He became quite hostile and I couldn't reason with him. Neither of us touched the holiday dinner I had prepared. I finally went up to bed closing the door so I wouldn't have to listen to the vulgar profanities. During our entire marriage he had never talked to me that way before. I dropped off to sleep and awoke to find him standing over me looking down at me with cold calculating eyes. He was very drunk and I honestly thought he was going to kill me. It was the first time I was ever afraid of him.

I thought he had returned to work after that weekend, but Heinz called to tell me he had been locked in his room for days drinking hard liquor and only leaving his bed to use the bathroom. Consequently, our son Chris drove his Dad back to our home in Palmdale. I recall Chris' big brown eyes looking at me hurtful wanting to know, *"Who is this guy you're seeing?"* I'll never forget that look, because it hurt more than all those past years of anxiety and loneliness. It was a long time before Chris understood there was more to the story than met the naked eye.

After Chris left that day Dave complained that his heart was *acting up* and I took him to the emergency clinic. The doctor told him he was in very poor physical condition. I didn't want things to be this way. It took a few days for him to detox and I helped him get back on his feet, without many words between us. We didn't discuss our situation and he returned to work taking the food I had prepared for him for the coming week. I wasn't sure what was coming next, but soon found out.

That week when I tried to use my gas credit card, they confiscated it. Our joint checking account was closed and Dave wasted no time to cancel me as the beneficiary on his life insurance policy. I had no money except for what I earned at my part-time job, so I asked for more hours. All very humiliating to show me he was the one in control of it all while I realized I had never really been in control of my own life. I even had to ask for grocery money so I could cook for him on the weekends. He didn't seem to care that I had no money to live on during the week.

That Christmas in our new house would be our last together as a family, although there was not much feeling of togetherness left. Dave and I had decided we would try to make it as nice a Christmas as possible in our lovely new home. I had always dreamed of owning a two-story home and as I had always imagined, I decorated the house with winding green garland on the staircase banister.

We went looking for a tree together, as we always had every year for the past twenty seven years. This one was especially beautiful and he helped me string the lights. Whendy and Drake and Chris came to Palmdale and we all went through the disengaging gestures of opening gifts and eating the special buffet I had prepared. This Christmas brought back the sad memories of the year before, when Brigitte was dying. Only this time it was our marriage and we knew it was our last Christmas together and as the year before it all seemed like a bad dream.

The following January 25th an apathetic Process Server handed me divorce papers at my work. I was stunned, as I had no idea Dave had filed for divorce and assumed that probably we would first separate for a time. I retained an attorney who advised me to draw some money on a credit card, which hadn't yet been canceled. This transaction at the bank made me feel like I was committing a crime. I found myself looking around nervously with sweaty palms and my heart pounding as I waited for the teller to call for an authorization. What could happen next?

Dave had been quite a busy detective. With John's phone number off our phone bill, he had a friend trace his number to his residence. Dave then drove to Lake Elizabeth, and posing as an insurance adjuster he questioned the neighbors who wondered about this intoxicated man who came to their door with a camera hanging from his neck, who then took photos of John's house and old cars. While I was at work on the weekends, Dave had placed a monitoring device in our attic on our phone line to trace and record my conversations. He intended to use all this evidence against me in court for the divorce proceedings, proving infidelity or a so-called adultery. He didn't realize that all his undercover work was in vain as the sordid evidence he produced was not valid evidence in the case of California law.

I received several snapshots in the mail, which Dave had secretly taken when he was stalking me. These always arrived without any note in a plain brown envelope. At that time he used any hurtful tactic he could think of to retaliate. It took a legal written letter to Dave's attorney from my attorney to cease his harassment and threats, which went on for quite some time. My friends at work warned me to be careful and to be aware of what was happening around me.

On February 15, 1990 my half-brother Hans-Dieter called me from Germany for my birthday. It was the last time I would ever hear from him. I knew he was very ill and I didn't tell him that Dave and I were separating or that I was in the process of packing and moving out. He passed away three weeks later on March 6; he would have been 46 the following October. My siblings were dying and leaving me to feel very alone.

Two days later I moved into a nice one-bedroom apartment not knowing how I was going to manage financially. All alone, for the first time in my life I realized a major portion had been missing from my life. I needed to find out who I really was, and to do that - most importantly I needed to know who my father was. Among the pictures I was about to display in my new home, I came across the one of my father which Brigitte had given to me at age 13, before I left for America. Within me I heard that voice which touched the deepest part of my soul: *"This is a part of who you are, and you must get it back."* It wouldn't be the last time that I would hear this voice of authority. I knew what I needed to do. I placed my father's photo into a silver frame, giving it the significance I thought it finally deserved. He had been nothing more to me than this picture - two dimensional, colorless, a shameful secret to be kept hidden. But now he was displayed with love, no longer a shameful secret, hidden from the world. But this was only the beginning, as I set out to find my "roots" and probe into my family's history.

The upcoming phase of my life was the beginning of my journey from secrecy to openness, from shunning the past to embracing it and from self-denial to self-awareness. Sometimes this was very frightening because now I was on my own for the first time in my life. I was suddenly thrown out into the real world with all the emotions of an inexperienced, vulnerable nineteen-year-old who had come from her parent's controlling home to the sheltered, secure world within my 28-year marriage.

It meant starting at the bottom - I had to establish credit for myself, which was not going to be easy since I never had any of my own. Dave made it very clear he did not want me to keep his family name and I immediately assumed a new legal name. Amazingly, it was not as difficult to obtain my own credit as I had feared. I received several credit cards which sometimes even paid my rent before my divorce was final. This

new independence was quite an adventure, but the uncertainty of my
future was still a little frightening. I had never had my *very own*
apartment and it was actually fun to set up my new home. It was cozy, but
if John hadn't been part of my life I would probably have been lost.

I had a car accident on Easter of that year. I was coming from
Lake Elizabeth at 8:00am having to work later that day in Palmdale. They
told me a ruptured tire caused me to roll five times, landing upside down
in the weeds at the side of the road. It all happened in slow motion as I
started to spin before I blacked out. When I came to, I was hanging
upside down still strapped in my seat belt.

The pretty card and Easter basket full of colored eggs, which John
had given me that morning, were scattered everywhere. I remember
calling for him, afraid when I saw that I was trapped in my car. We really
were kindred spirits and very much in tune because a few minutes later he
was there holding me, comforting me. He had been on his way to Los
Angeles when something told him to take the other route through
Palmdale. He said when he came around the curve and saw my car upside
down he thought *"God no, I just found her!"*

I only had a broken finger and a severe concussion, which caused
my entire head to swell twice its size, not a pretty sight! However, John
was there to take care of me and I recovered. I recall he made me a grilled
cheese sandwich at my apartment which I forced down not wanting to hurt
his feelings.

Sometime later I even bought myself another car. But while I was
without transportation it was John who drove the seventeen miles one way
from Lake Elizabeth to Palmdale every day to take me to work and then
returned at night to pick me up. Needless to say, he spent a great deal of
time at my apartment with me and we became very close.

On December 29th at 4:00am a fire raged at John's house, although
contained to only one room. He showed up at my apartment soon
afterward with his fingers badly burned. The following day he received a
call telling him his mother in Colorado had passed away at 4:00am that
same morning. I used my credit card and we both flew to Colorado for the

funeral. He said he wanted me there with him, but when he insisted to stop over in Las Vegas and asked to gamble with my credit card, I was startled and it should have been an indication of what was to come.

It seemed, every day I was learning something new. Although I was now working full time I was grateful to have the credit cards as my job at the dress shop didn't pay well. I discovered that I could get *cash advances* at the then fairly newfound *ATM* machines. One day while I was at work on a break I thought I would give this a test. I was in a grocery store waiting in line observing the people in front of me. When my turn came I followed the given directions, inserting my card, punching in my pin number. I then waited with much anticipation, and I waited and waited but no money came out.

I will never forget the expression on the face of the man standing behind me, when I turned to him shrugging my shoulders, asking him very puzzled *"Where's the money?"* It was a very funny incident, but I must admit it was the innocence of who I was at that point in time which told the whole story. When I told the women at work they roared with laughter. I was learning life's little lessons but the ATM machine was the funniest. It seems I had used the wrong card. Often I still wonder *"Where's the money?"* and have to smile.

Since it was I who had a new *lover,* people assumed that I was the cause for the break-up and Dave was the *poor jilted husband. He* played the part well. But it was of my own doing due to the fact I had done such a great job of *enabling* and *covering up*, something I learned to do long ago as a child. How then could anyone have known how we both had suffered the anguish in our own personal ways, the results caused by his alcoholism? Looking back today there are things I wish I had done differently, but it was never my intention to hurt anyone. We both had drifted apart years before when his flirtation began with the bottle, which soon consumed him entirely.

But the greatest hurt and disappointment came when I realized I had not only lost my friends, but also my family. My children were going through their own pain of our separation. Their Dad was very influential and did his best to discredit me and for a time he succeeded. All those years I thought I was protecting them, but now it had only led to their confusion and misunderstanding. It was the repeated pattern in my life - secrets -just as I had kept my own past from my children. I had become an expert at personal subterfuge - hiding the facts of my life - deftly evading questions and always covering up the truth.

Yes, my life was going to change in many respects, but the rude awakening came when I realized that the people who had been my family for twenty-eight years no longer cared and had chosen sides.

We had many great times with Dave's sister Sally, her husband and their children M and D. Sally was like my sister, the fun loving, crazy red head that I called *"Lucy"*. Her daughter was getting married and I wondered why I hadn't received my invitation. It was the final humiliating dismissal the day Sally called me at my apartment. *"Bobbie, I need to talk to you but this is going to be so difficult for me. I have to ask you not to come to M's wedding. Dave will not participate if you're going to show up."*

I swallowed hard fighting back the tears and emotion and could only say, *"OK."* I was in complete shock. I thought they were my family? Just the year before Sally wrote in my birthday card, *"You are a very, very special person who brings a lot of love and sunshine into our lives."* It didn't matter that I had already purchased and sent the set of fine crystal goblets - chosen with much love – as a wedding gift for my niece who was also my godchild. It was with even greater amazement when my own daughter Whendy gave her opinion of why I shouldn't have been there. She said, *"How do you think Dad would have felt?"* No one seemed to understand.

They had now all closed their doors to me, something I honestly never expected. Ron, my brother-in-law, stopped answering my notes but I could still hear him say to me before our separation, *"Bobbie, no matter what happens between you and Dave you'll always be part of our family."* They were my family for so long, it was and still is difficult to let go. Today Sally and I exchange birthday cards and I hear from Ron at Christmas time. What I feel for them will never change.

I realized by finally finding some happiness, I also had many sacrifices to make. There were accusations and gossip and looks that needed no words. But that was all part of breaking away and making new beginnings. No, it was too late to reconcile too much distress for too long, and besides, there now was John. Later I often secretly wondered how it would have been had we worked things out.

Dave finally agreed to let me have the Christmas decorations, which meant a great deal to me, even dropping them off at my apartment. But when I went to set up my cherished porcelain Nativity Scene the following Christmas, I understood the reason for his so eager generosity. There was an empty space in the box, which held Mary, Joseph and child. Joseph the father was missing. Dave knew this would be the ultimate statement leaving a profound message, and he thereby had the last laugh, but unfortunately nobody was laughing! For me it signified the void of Dave in my life from then on.

Our divorce was final on March 5, 1991. Dave and I left the Ventura courthouse, both of us parting in tears going our separate ways. But the harsh reality of our separation would not fully penetrate until the following day when I suddenly realized that our 28 years together were now only memories.

I still hear the last words he spoke to me on that day of February 17, 1990 as I was moving out of our house on Riviera Court. I walked outside into the falling snow and climbed into the moving van when he called to me *"Have a nice Life!*

Divorce is death. I'll never really get over it.

Chapter 8. A new Beginning leads to the Past

On April 4, 1991 at my apartment sitting on my small balcony I wrote:

"I just watched John drive away, the top down and his blonde hair blowing wild in the wind. I waved until he disappeared in the distance on the freeway. He looked so good...I love him so very much, even though there are so many questions, doubts and insecurities still within me! Sometimes I have to wonder about my life and what I'm doing here alone in a small apartment?"

When John had told me *"I'll take you places you've never been!"* I had no idea then that meant living on the edge for the next fourteen years of my life.

We were spending more time together than we were apart. John had been making that drive back and forth from Lake Elizabeth to Palmdale every day for four months before I was able to buy another car.

He told me he knew of a vacant home in Lake Los Angeles, an area about twenty miles south of Palmdale; the owners were living in Hawaii and we could move in together. I wasn't too enthusiastic over the idea, although I wanted to be with him. It would be quite a distance from my work and I wondered how we could make it financially. At this point John still had a few of his former pool maintenance accounts in Beverly Hills and he was also trying to get his film projects off the ground. He said, *"I'll even get another job of some kind if I have to!"* Consequently, for some time we stayed afloat on a very limited income.

On Memorial Day before we moved into the house in Lake Los Angeles, John picked me up after work and we took the picnic I had prepared. We had already painted the entire interior of the home a fresh shade of white and generally cleaned everything. On the patio in the backyard we improvised, making a table by placing a board across an old porcelain bathroom fixture that was left there and I laid the checkered red tablecloth on top of it. There we enjoyed our first romantic dinner at our new home. What fun we had that day on the quiet desert as we stayed to watch the magnificent desert sunset!

Lake Los Angeles is a remote desert area consisting of nice but modest, affordable homes on better than half acre lots. There was already a full grown willow tree in the front yard and John landscaped creating a large heart which he outlined with existing rocks. Within the heart he planted flowers, all for me he told me. He planted Italian cypress lining the driveway and honeysuckle bushes surrounding the low fence around the entire front yard. He had spotted a huge decorative hollow log in a nearby empty lot. I was stunned and realized his strength when I saw him walking toward our house carrying this log across his shoulders as if he was Paul Bunyon.

In the backyard he built a wall of bottles, all sorts, colors and sizes surrounding the patio where the suns' rays reflected through the bottles casting unique abstract patterns on the patio floor. He planted several willow trees and built a wooden deck from pallets he found where I loved to sit with Mozel and Rosebud, John's dog and cat. From this deck there was a magnificent view of vast open plains with only some Joshua Cactus Trees scattered throughout the panorama.

The desert sunsets were spectacular and I used to visualize the twenty mule team wagons making their way across the prairie. All this beauty was however shared with the other occupants of the living desert like rabbits, lizards, scorpions, vinegaroons, black widow spiders and noisy large black ravens.

We loved the wide-open spaces and the feeling of freedom. John has a genuine fondness for birds filling our many feeders daily and then calling them with *"Birdie Yum Yum!"* They always came flying when they heard his call.

I was soon transferred to the Lancaster store a few short miles from Palmdale and was made assistant manager. In October 1991 Miranda was born to Drake and Whendy. She was a beautiful child looking much like her mother used to. She called me *"Omi"*. When she was two years old was one of the few times I was asked to take care of her while Drake and Whendy went away for a weekend.

Windsor the Fashion Boutique where I had worked since my move to Palmdale went out of business and closed their doors in January 1993. I already had started the preliminaries to writing my family's history and John encouraged me to stay home and work on my book full time. I realize today that these years with John, which have often been unsettling and filled with insecurities, were nevertheless my given opportunity to turn all my attention to writing which much later came to be *The Auschwitz Kommandant*. I don't know if I would have been able to accomplish it had I gone back to work. However, I was worried about the loss of income, but agreed to stay home, and it was then I encountered *"the voice in the closet"*. With the onset of my research and writing, my life would soon be changed forever.

Living together was quite a transition and challenge for both John and me. He was definitely a free spirit and had been a bachelor without responsibilities or commitments for too long, although I wasn't asking for commitment or even marriage, as I don't think I ever want to marry again. Spending considerable time together day after day also was an adjustment and I didn't find it amusing when he rearranged my kitchen. I had to come to an understanding that he was a man unlike anyone I had been accustomed to, who also took an interest in the kitchen and I had to learn to share! We both love nature and I especially adored the closeness when he read to me in bed at night and his fingers worked magic on my headaches. He often told me *"We've got it all, it doesn't get any better than this!"* Those were the times I loved him with all my heart. Oh, but he really had been a challenge and I often wondered if I had made a big mistake or should have stayed in my apartment. But there is a reason for everything they say? My life now centered on the research into my past and the writing of my book.

Under the false illusion of what appeared as renewed happiness to me my life actually had gone from bad to worse. There had been warning signs, which I didn't heed, and soon my existence was spinning out of control. John didn't find another job as he promised and I was heading down a path where there was not enough money coming in. I was desperately trying to pay the bills. John thought he was very close to getting one of his projects off the ground. He was dealing with some Russian producers on a ballet film production. After all the time, work and even money invested again his dream never materialized.

I often had to use my credit cards to buy groceries. It was like I was caught in a tailspin and no way to end the vicious cycle. The creditors were hounding me and I was devastated that the credit, which I had established and earned for myself with so much pride, was ruined in a matter of two years.

In September of 1993 with great humiliation I had to file for bankruptcy. John suggested if I let him take over my checkbook, he could fix everything! I told him that will never happen as his "help" got us into this predicament in the first place. I will never forget the generosity of my friend Brenda at this time who was going through terrible hardships herself, but who shared food items, often sending me home with bags that had been donated to her by her church.

Dave remarried in December of 1993.

On January 17, 1994 at 4:30am we were awakened by the violent shaking of a destructive 6.6 earthquake. We lived near the path of the fault, but had no damage, although it caused tremendous loss nearby, including lives.

The following month in February John's adoptive mother Lila died, beginning a bitter legal battle which would last three years and took an emotional toll on him. As a result he lost land and property which had belonged to his family for generations. It was a drawn out period of delays and terrible frustration for him. He had hoped that the inheritance would have come forth in time to help yet another approaching predicament.

The owners of the house we were living in were John's family returning from Hawaii, and in October we were forced to move. I had packed everything I could, but not knowing what our future held at that point, I actually divided our belongings, separating our kitchen utensils and books. I really didn't know if this was the end of our relationship and at that point in time I wasn't sure why I would want to stay. John waited until the day before they were expected to return and then he finally began packing up his room. I stayed up the night before helping him pack and we were still putting things into boxes when the owners arrived and proceeded to move in on top of us. John must have kept every item he ever owned in his entire life, never getting rid of anything. It was a nightmare to pack all his things but worse still, where would we go with all this *stuff*? We had no money.

The house next door came available and we stacked all our boxes on the driveway. I called to have the utilities transferred next door and felt relieved as we waited for the key to the home. But my feelings of contentment were premature as at the last moment the woman decided she wasn't going to rent her house after all.

Now it all makes sense, as I wondered how could we rent? Where would it come from? There we were, our belongings on the driveway and no place to go. I was gripped with panic. These were unbelievable circumstances and we were now homeless street people. It was much worse than having been a refugee as a child because then I was unaware of what was happening. This was very real!

We ended up sleeping in John's van, parked in their side yard, while the owners were comfortable in their bedroom inside the house which used to be ours only the day before. They let us set up our coffee maker in their garage where all our furniture was now stacked, plugged in on top of my washing machine. The joy of a cup of coffee in the morning was one thing I was not ready to give up.

I quickly learned the feelings which homeless people must have to endure, feelings of lowest self-esteem and worthlessness. I tried to pretend I was camping again but this was one adventure in my life I could have done without.

They did let us use their bathroom, but made us feel very unwelcome when we came into their house, which now looked like a cyclone had blown through it. Before they returned I had scrubbed every room and even left them some flowers out of the yard in the kitchen. I can't remember when I experienced such despair and hopelessness. I had now sunk to the lowest form of human existence. How could I have let this happen to me? I knew feeling sorry for myself, and the tears wouldn't help, but I felt like a child wanting her mother.

And it was mother who came to the rescue, Ursula and her husband Jesse came through with a loan. Mom had been very morally supportive since my divorce, but then she never really liked Dave and now she was there for me. However they never knew how bad things really were. No one did. It would have been too humiliating to tell my family I was living on the street.

We, including the dog and cat, lived in the van and did most of our eating in the garage for about three weeks. For me it all transpired like a daydream, a detached state of mind where I could only cope with this way of existence.

John found a cabin in Wrightwood, which is a beautiful mountain skiing community approximately twenty miles from where we were in Lake Los Angeles. John liked the charming small wooden cabin, I didn't. It was gloomy. We were cramped with our bed in the living room and the second bedroom was our storage area for the *stuff.* There was no garage. The washer and dryer were outdoors in an open air shed and it was quite an adventure to do my laundry in the snow. I cleaned and disinfected the entire place but the odor that an intruding bear had left previously, never went away. But at least we had a roof over our heads. Just the same we were outsiders to the people who lived around us. We didn't belong. At least, I didn't feel this is where I was meant to be.

Even farther away from civilization, we now had to leave the mountain for most of our needs. The transmission on my car broke down and we could never depend on John's cars. I will never forget the day we drove off the mountain into town when we were suddenly caught in a terrible rainstorm along the most treacherous section of the highway. His windshield wipers quit working, cutting off all visibility to the road in front of us. I began hyperventilating and thought I would pass out with fear. Somehow we made it back home, but the ordeal continued.

The next six months were a living nightmare; still no money. We literally lived on popcorn on a daily basis. I used olive oil on my face in place of moisturizing cream and did without those necessities, which I had always taken for granted. Sometimes we couldn't even afford a pound of coffee and that was the ultimate sacrifice. I would have been eligible for food stamps, but that was an option which I never considered. I was too proud. However, at the grocery store I watched in amazement the number of people who paid for their loaded shopping carts precisely this way, using the state as their crutch.

What little money we had we saved for gasoline to get us to town. We walked the mile to the post office every day, which took us through this lovely area that I would have really appreciated at any other time under normal circumstances. My God, what was I doing here with him?

Christmas came and I put up a small tree. My *JC Penney* charge account was the only credit card I still had and it made it possible to purchase gifts for my family on special occasions, also necessary shoes and clothing when we needed them. It was a far cry from my chic boutique fashions. *JC Penney* will never know how wonderful it was to have the availability and luxury of shopping their catalogue.

My children came for Christmas and I cooked Spaghetti. They were used to their mother's holiday feasts, so this was a first. We all slept in our one main room and I felt very claustrophobic, but it wasn't only the cabin which was closing in on me. Whendy and Chris were not aware of our desperate circumstances at that time, but I know they sensed something was wrong. It was a terribly depressing holiday for me, but they all seemed to have fun and Miranda played in the snow.

Every day on the mountain I had a painful headache compounded by a nagging toothache, and the only way to get warm was to crawl into our waterbed in our living room. John and I were both starting to feel the unhealthy aftereffects of a steady diet of popcorn. I really tried not to let things get me down and kept reminding myself of my favorite motto when things got tough, *"It's only temporary!"* and knowing that was true got me through another day.

Another rude awakening came to me when I discovered John was donating $50 to his favorite ministry, the Reverend Ike charities. It was these type of donations that contributed to the Reverend's fleet of Cadillac's and his luxurious lifestyle. That $50 could have bought us some real food. I knew he considered it "seed money", but I just couldn't understand his thinking. I was furious, disappointed and knew something had to change.

Heinz called me on my birthday on February 15th 1995. He asked, *"Little one, are you happy?"* He sensed something was wrong, but I couldn't tell him the truth. I made up some lame excuse and tried to sound happy. I missed him much more than he knew and the strength in his voice and that familiar German accent almost caused me to fall apart. It also made me realize how isolated I was from my family. It was our last contact. Heinz died suddenly on February 24th. After that I really felt like everyone from my past had left me. Things could be worse, but how much more could I take? Ironically at his funeral someone asked me if I was still a *gourmet cook*?

In the meantime I was writing a book. Throughout all the adversity I never stopped. It had become my life's passion, the one incentive that kept me going. My inspiration was always renewed at those times when I looked at my father's handsome photo and I could almost hear him tell me that through his influence - even now - his blessings would soon turn my life around so *"**Don't give up!**"* ...and I didn't.

I had written the very first draft in pencil, then typed the entire manuscript before a friend Marji transposed it onto her computer. Before I began I had translated both Journals which were the letters my father wrote to his second wife Anneliese during the years of 1945-1947 while he was a POW of the Americans at Dachau. It was a very emotionally draining task. Another source of important information was the cassette tapes recorded by my sister Brigitte before she died, providing significant facts about our family. It was all highly inspiring material.

While in Wrightwood I sent out the first query letters to numerous publishers for the draft I had just completed. I barely scraped together enough money for the postage. Our walk to the post office every day was with great expectation of what news I might receive. Most of the answers were rejections, but one publisher did ask to see my manuscript only to return it with regrets. I was slowly learning the ways of the publishing world, but most of all I came to the realization that these people were not receptive to a story about a Nazi Kommandant. It was kindly suggested by one of the publishers that I contact Literary Agents. At the library I found a recent list of agents and again sent out numerous query letters.

My sister Antje married Ernst that year and finally found happiness after years of her own hardships.

John's dog Mozel died that February adding to our misery. Wrightwood was a terribly dark time for both of us.

In May we moved to Lake Elizabeth, with a most generous offer from Marji, a special friend of John's. Another friend loaned us his small home-made trailer with which John made about eight trips over seventy miles one way, moving everything himself. It's a wonder he even had the strength because he was very run down at this point. We both lost some of our muscle tone from the lack of proper nutrition. Neither of us could even look at popcorn for a long time after that.

Marji's house was bright and cheerful and I felt like a dark cloud had suddenly been lifted. I was once more full of hope that a fresh new beginning was awaiting us. Now I could concentrate on my book and the headaches miraculously improved.

Today it is actually snowing and very cold! The only way we've kept warm is to bundle up in layers of clothing or turn on the oven. We have no firewood and I have even slipped back into our heated waterbed for a few moments at a time to thaw out. Life since my divorce has been extremely difficult by having made some bad choices, but I'm working hard on improving my future.

We now live in Lake Elizabeth, a picturesque small, quaint high desert community of rolling hills, covered by chaparral, sage and bright orange California poppies in the springtime. Lake Elizabeth is about 80 miles from Los Angeles. We're at an elevation of 3200' with a population of approximately 500 people. There are two lakes: the smaller of the two is Lake Hughes, and large old cottonwood trees surround both, which display lovely hues of gold in the autumn. The white blossoms of the honey locus trees flurry in the wind in late springtime, leaving heaps of sweet fragrant petals by the roadside.

Lake Elizabeth was named in 1850 by members of a wagontrain which was headed to the gold country, making their way through the San Joaquin valley. Even today the area has not changed too much throughout the years, almost as though it had been caught in a time warp. There is no town to speak of; the area consists primarily of the new residential homes, many of them overlooking the lake, but also contrasted with some of the remaining old original cabins.

There is a grade school, a few churches of various denominations, a golf course with the original club house built 100 years ago, the Lucky Days Bar and the Lake Hughes Post Office. There are no major stores of any kind, only *Papa's* small country store, which carries the basic items. A plaque on Lake Elizabeth road is one of several historic remains depicting the former site of the local hotel which was once a stage coach stop. Sometimes we go for a treat and allow ourselves a great hamburger at the *Rock House Inn Bed & Breakfast* which was once also a stagecoach stop as well as the Post Office and General Store, with its rustic wooden floors and an ornate old western style bar. It's exterior is faced entirely with river rock built in 1929 and represents the charm of that era.

The legend of our very own "Loch Ness" Monster was believed to be haunting Lake Elizabeth as far back as the mid 1800's when that first wagon train camped on its shore. In March 1928, in the near-by San Francisquito canyon, the walls of the St. Francis Dam, then a vital part of the distant Los Angeles water and power system, gave way, carrying with it its helpless victims, as well as bridges and structures across the Santa Clara Valley. Like our snowfall today the summers become equally severe with temperatures soaring past the 100's.

Lake Elizabeth is almost a bit of a Peyton Place where everyone knows everyone else. I am probably the exception because I have been a total recluse since John and I moved here in 1995. My days are spent in front of the computer working on my book. The only contact with the outside world has been through the small window that looks out onto the street, which is next to my work area. From here I can observe my neighbors and watch the cars speed up and down the street past our house.

An occasional hungry coyote roams the foothills across the road from which vantage point several large two-story homes look down on us from the top of a high ridge. A covey of fat little quail occasionally come to visit in the front yard, and the many birds, including the tiny colorful Hummingbirds, are always at the various feeders outside of our kitchen window.

I have become very aware and in tune with what is going on around me. The happy sounds of summertime, is carried through the voices of the children next door, splashing in their pool calling ..*Marco-Polo,* while the younger ones imitate their mothers, preparing afternoon tea parties for their dolls. They are happy sounds but almost haunting echoes from the past, as I find myself reliving the fond memories of the good times I had shared with my own children so long ago. In the summertime hundreds of cottonwood seeds looking like tiny fairies carried by the wind - drift aimlessly past my window, while busy black bumblebees buzz around the tall sunflowers.

During my writing I have come to know the habits of the people around me. The times they leave in the mornings and return at the end of each day. Those times at the end of the day just like clockwork are usually my cues to take a break and think about preparing dinner. I always wished them all a safe journey through the winding canyon, especially when it rained or snowed. Of course they never knew that within the seclusion of my cozy office, they actually became a very real part of my isolated world. I really have kept to myself which probably raises many questions around the neighborhood.

Sometimes a whole week passes by here without hearing a word from anyone, quite isolated, but I have almost become used to it and it is very conducive to searching one's soul and creative writing.

Only the good-natured women working at our small Lake Hughes Post Office know of me. They so often assist me with the confusing and involved mailings of endless queries and literary material, which I sent to agents and publishers everywhere. They have shared an interest in the possibility that one of these days my book could actually be published. Of course, time and again the same SAS Envelopes which they helped me to weigh and prepare with return postage, would eventually come back rejected, ending up being stuffed back into my own PO Box by them. They have long since stopped inquiring about my progress.

Shortly after writing to some literary agents, I received a phone call from one of them. He worked with a producer and they were interested in my project for a movie-of-the- week story. The producer himself contacted me and I found out his mother was well known in the world of literary fiction. He saw my book as one of those glitzy Hollywood sagas. It was my first introduction to that element of show business and I also realized the animosity that was still very obvious on the subject of Nazism, notably the fact that my father had been a Kommandant at a concentration camp.

My discussion that day with this man was interesting and certainly an eye opener as to what was in store for me in order to get my story told. I also realized that I had much more research to do to be able to answer questions for which I really had no explanations at that point. They referred me to an English Professor in the San Francisco area who could help me with my writing. Jann was also a published author and we hit it off immediately. She suggested in addition to my father's story that it should be more autobiographical and I then proceeded to rewrite a second draft.

Jann was soft-spoken, yet her writing had incredible strength. I admired her literary genius and she quickly became my mentor. She corrected the new pages and found the many commas I had injected throughout my manuscript especially comical. She volunteered her assistance giving me the guidance I needed and I respected her knowledge and embraced her as a much-needed teacher and caring new friend.

In the meantime I continued with my extensive research. I spent much time at the library looking for and reading books on the topic of World War II or anything on Nazi Germany. I found my father mentioned in several of these. I bought all the new books that were published on the subject and contacted the authors, some as far away as Canada and England. From England came the addresses of numerous historical archives where I found valuable information on my father.

The Auschwitz State Museum was of tremendous help and I was very grateful for their willingness to assist me. The actual transcripts from father's trial in Krakow were written in Polish and translated by Karl Morys, a friend of my sisters'. Many other German documents had to be translated into English. I received documentation of my father's SS File from the National Archives in Washington DC and I sent for two microfilms which consisted of the transcripts of his testimony at the Nuremberg pre trial interrogations of war criminals. I even found a sound recording of the same. This was extremely moving for me, as I had never heard my father's voice.

When I came across an interesting article written by history Professor Robert Barr Smith in a World War II Magazine about the Nuremberg Trials, I knew I needed to contact him. When he heard my story, he called it *"A Bittersweet Journey"*, which was to become the new working title for my next draft, which I assumed would be the final draft.

Professor Smith, who is also a published author, was kind enough to read and evaluate my manuscript and suggested (as I myself had always felt) that the story should depict my father as the central figure. He said he found it very interesting and his personal opinion of a story about my father was: *"It is a story of a decent man caught in a very bad place who did the best he could under the circumstances."*

Unfortunately, when I told Jann of my intentions of changing the premise and going back to my original draft, she was very upset with me. I was truly sorry that I disappointed her, but I too was disappointed as I thought that she had believed in the story of my father. Besides, I really questioned who would be interested in my own personal insignificant story? She told me that no one would be interested or share my enthusiasm for a story about a man who *chose* to become a Nazi and member of the SS. Her words still haunt me, *"You will run into a tidal wave of opposition!"*

For sometime after that I was beginning to think she was right. Sadly it ended our professional relationship, but not for long. As for me, she would always be a friend and I shall never forget the help and support she provided. She especially gave me confidence to continue when she told me I was a good writer. It was all part of my learning experience and every day brought me closer to the end results. I continued with my relentless quest, even more determined than ever that I would succeed.

The research and writing was a daily routine. Sometimes I thought of things in the middle of the night and rose to make notes of things I might otherwise forget. I really felt that the drive within me came from another dimension. I sensed the force was my father and the *"voice"* was always within me.

Our life in Lake Elizabeth was quiet except for the stormy times in our relationship, although John seldom complained about me spending all my time in front of the computer or my constant reading, studying, researching or translating. I became entirely absorbed into that time in history and the story of my past and family gradually unfolded. But noticeably not without extreme mental exhaustion, which I realize was also not easy on John.

Sometimes I had to tune out his 1950's rock and roll music or even plug my ears in order to concentrate on my writing. I could hardly expect him to stop living, since there was nowhere to escape to in this small house. We always worked through it somehow and often he would just go to soak in a soothing hot bath of vinegar and Indian Clay, listening to his motivational tapes.

The first Christmas in this house was much better for us than the one we had survived in Wrightwood, but our finances had not yet improved. I found a small 5' artificial tree which had been left behind in the garage. We still had no money for a real tree, but I so wanted to get into the holiday spirit. I've never had anything but a fresh tree, but it's amazing what we can do when we have no other choices. John was not home and I decided to surprise him.

When I put this tree together it looked pitiful, much like the one in the *Charlie Brown* cartoon. Listening to Christmas music, I put the finishing touches and final decorations on the tree and lit the lights, I had to sit down and cry with joy. It was absolutely beautiful and hardly noticeable that it wasn't a genuine live pine tree. John too loved our little tree and I have since put it up every year.

The cold season of February 1997 was of more lean times and once again things looked pretty bleak. My Journal reveals my ongoing struggle living with John:

Dear Diary:

"I am so cold my hands are stiff making it very difficult to write. There is no heat in the house. We are burning old furniture out of the Garage...

We are behind on the Electric bill.

The Propane Tank ran empty. Now I can't even use the stove to cook... but be that as it may there are no groceries anyway. The refrigerator is bare.

We are taking cold showers and today they also came to shut off the water.

Our car broke down leaving us without transportation and we have walked the six miles round-trip to pick up our mail at the Lake Hughes Post Office.

However, all that is really unimportant because this house is going into foreclosure! [where will I go?...I don't know!]

No, this is not over 50 years ago, although it seems I'm reliving some of my past.

I've been working frantically to finish my book, which I've written for you Papa....my gift to you with all my love....Maybe the answer to my loneliness?
Sometimes I wonder how I've coped with all this for so long, and when will things begin to break?

Still to me life is wonderful, I have much to be grateful for and yes things could be worse! I have to find the humor in it all, even now.
I will win and my book will be published.....but alas my printer just ran out of ink!!!

This is true but who will ever believe it?..."

February 28, 1997
Barbara U. Cherish

Today I cooked bacon and eggs for John and served it to him on a tray in bed. [Again] I am starting to resent this and I didn't eat with him but took my shower instead. I have told him it is beginning to feel like I am living with an invalid. Very depressing that he spends so much time in bed. He says he's "studying" and the vibes are better in the bedroom, where he has several books, journals and the Bible spread out in front of him. Lately if he's not in bed then he is in his "museum" of a room, surrounded by some incredible memorabilia - dusty reminders from his past.

John was in one of his argumentative moods and I shouldn't have even talked to him because then he started in on me. Years earlier he tried to get me to say some affirmations with him at which time I tried to explain to him that I have my own beliefs and feelings within my soul. I pray by simply talking to my inner spirit. I don't like someone to force their beliefs on me.

It seems all John wants to do is pray. God, where is this going? I do believe a change is coming and definitely needed here. But I don't know how much longer I can hang in there?

He said, *"You resent my praying!"* I answered, *"I don't resent it, I just don't understand it, so I've let it go, realizing you have to do your own thing. You want togetherness which for me would be to talk about things that are of concern to me, without it always ending up in an argument."* He raised his voice, *"You don't know what I'm doing when I pray, it is also studying which helps me toward what I want to do!"* Shouting back at him in frustration I said, *"No I don't understand and I don't know if anyone could deal with someone like you John, who is constantly praying like a monk in a "friggin" monastery, that's why I'm concentrating on doing my own thing!"* Repeatedly slapping my right hand into my left palm, I try to bring my point across with great frustration. *"You can't just spend all of your time praying about it you have to apply yourself to make it happen!"* He actually laughed at that, saying that display of emotion would be a great scene for a movie script and he told me to write it down...?

When John's family settlement came through things improved financially for us for a time. John paid off many of our outstanding debts and even Ursula was paid back what she had loaned to us in 1994. Her husband Jesse passed away in 1998 and that year Mom, with the help of Jesse's son Randy, brought me her cherished Rosenthal and Cobalt china and crystal along with the china cabinet to keep them in. These same heirlooms go back to the days I was a foster child living in the American housing project in Fuerth-Nuremberg. Ursula had previously already handed down some paintings and other sentimental pieces which hold fond memories, including the silver knight which is the lighter and music box that plays the *Third Man* theme. She knew I would be the one to appreciate and care for these items and I do, more than she'll ever know. Randy had become an extended brother. He even gave me his old computer which I am still gratefully using today.

After they left that weekend and I happily unpacked the boxes. I was suddenly overwhelmed with a deep sense of tremendous loss. I felt as though Ursula was already gone. I wept as I unwrapped these lovely things which depicted another whole phase of my life, a time between us which wasn't always happy, but embodied with a love which endured even through many difficulties. More than that, it depicts a life from a time so long ago as I reminisce about these parents who chose to adopt a half grown girl and give her a chance of a life in America.

Throughout the difficult times which John and I encountered, Ursula brought us care packages of groceries and canned goods and sent us special bread from the German bakery. I don't know if she realized that was often our only source of food. I want her to know how much I appreciate her and love her and hopefully she will understand the reason I had to write this memoir.

I kept busy working on my book and as before my days evolved by returning to the past - living within the pages of my book manuscript - a place where I am never alone.

Chris and Mari were married on September 20, 1997. The month before they had a lovely bridal shower which included the men. My nephew Kye was there with his wife Kriste and son Nicholas. Kye invited John and me to come with them that night to spend the weekend at their beach house at the Oxnard marina. He told me he had purchased it after his Mother, my sister Brigitte, passed away and how the view of the ocean brought him closer to her.

It was wonderful watching the waves and I too felt the nearness to Brigitte that weekend and also to Kye. He went out the next morning before breakfast and returned with a pink toothbrush for me. I still have it, as I have held on to the unforgettable memories of that special time with him that weekend. But the painful memories of my sister's burial at sea all returned to remind me she was gone forever.

Living within this decent hard working young man is still a lonely little boy grieving for his deceased parents. I sensed his loneliness and felt such incredible empathy. Kye's looks are from the Liebehenschel side and there is a quiet but deep family bond between us.

Chris and Mari's wedding was lovely. His uncle Father Ron - my former brother-in-law, performed the ceremony in Thousand Oaks, just as he had married his own brother and me. He also married his sister Sally, his niece Whendy and he had also baptized all of the children as well as officiating at his parents' Ruby and Johnny's funerals.

After arranging for a motel room in Thousand Oaks, we were walking out through the front door when Ron happened to be going in. He continued walking right past me. I called to him, *"Ron!"*. He stopped and looked at me puzzled, but after a moment he finally recognized me. We hugged but it was awkward and I was touched with a strange sense of profound sadness and loss. I didn't realize my now blonde hair had made that much difference or how much time had passed and how our lives had changed.

Dave sat at the opposite side of the Banquet room with his new wife and his brother Ron at his table. He chose to ignore me, but with considerable difficulty and dignity I paid my respects at their table. Dave never looked up or acknowledged that I was even there. Back at our table I fought back the tears.

I sat with our old friends, Boyce and Mary Jane and Betty, whose husband Don had been best man at our wedding and had passed away in 1992. They had all been at our wedding thirty-five years earlier. Today they were also staying at the same motel and we had a chance to be together. Boyce's words still haunt me as he looked at me from across the table and he simply stated: *"Let it go!"* He was wise, never wasting any words and he was so right.

Boyce passed away in August of 1999. I will miss him always. Whendy sat at a table with her in-laws and was hurtfully distant that day. I don't know, why but I felt sorry for Dave that all of *our* friends, who were actually his friends before I knew them, sat with me at my table.

Two days after Chris' wedding Kye called to tell me that the dreaded test results the doctor had recently taken of his lymph glands had come back positive. He found out the Friday before the wedding and had kept the devastating diagnosis of Lymphoma to himself, not wanting to spoil the festivities. No one had any idea. The phone line went deadly silent in my total disbelief. I was gripped with an instant sinking feeling and sickening fear. It all came rushing back as I recalled seventeen years earlier when his mother, my sister Brigitte told me of her diagnosis of breast cancer. Suddenly I found myself reliving that pain and heard her expressing her deepest feelings for her only son *"I love him so much I can't bear the thought of leaving him!"*

I felt as though my own heart would break and I wished I could have taken him into my arms to tell him everything would be all right. I also knew this was no time to give up and after a dreadful week in the depth of depression and despondency, I managed to pull myself together once again.

As of today Kye is doing very well and planning another trip to Europe in June. Unfortunately he was forced to sell his beach house. In 1998 Kye contributed a generous gift toward my plane ticket, initiating my trip to Germany after 26 years which was a loving gift from John. This journey to the past was the research needed for the completion of my book, revisiting with family, friends and highlighted by the incredible tour through the Auschwitz concentration camp.

Through my research in 1997, I came upon the book *"Menschen in Auschwitz"* written by Holocaust survivor Hermann Langbein. He had been a prisoner at Auschwitz the same time my father was Kommandant. He wrote extensively of his contact with my father. I wrote to his widow who in turn referred me to other survivors. Among them was Sonja Fischmann Fritz, whom my father had actually hired as a clerk. She worked in his office of the *Kommandantur* from January to May 1944. Sonja Fritz wrote to me recalling that her memory of my father was that of *"a good human being"*. I was elated to have her given statement. Dr. Janusz Mlynarski was another survivor whom I contacted and was fortunate enough to meet while on my trip. The interview with him was of tremendous interest for the completion of my book.

Consequently my need and perseverance to write my book all seemed to come together after years of tenacious work. It was with patient research and with the guidance of the *voice within me* that I was able to compile the important facts and learn about my family.

This *Sequel*, however, came primarily through the black and white images within my own mind, vivid scenes which have remained an unforgettable outline of my past.

It is Memorial Day 2000 and all of the lovely signs of spring have long vanished, taking with it the sweet smell of the blooming lilacs whose fragrance had drifted so seductively through the open window in my office. The blossoming honeysuckle have now replaced the lilacs with their own lovely fragrance, while the lush green hillsides surrounding us have turned into the familiar, golden dry landscape of summer. The days are becoming warmer. Once again the attentive sparrows, high up in our Italian Cypress trees, have hatched their eggs and the fledglings are now leaving the nest, flying past my window as they have done every spring the previous five years.

.....And so life continues...

June 1, 2000...Dear Diary

As this Sequel is winding towards the end I am still waiting for things to progress on my book. If only the phone would ring and I would hear that my project is finally on its way .I am still hopeful and feel everything will work out even though my days of waiting have been filled with questions and apprehension.

Things have been remarkably mellow around our house however and like a ray of sunshine John came home today with a smiling face, surprising me with a flat of luscious red ripe strawberries, roasted chicken, fresh donuts and a beautiful bouquet of pink carnations. "I thought you needed something to cheer you!" he said... still there is no word about our pending move...

June 12... It is 8:00am, the long yellow school bus stopped in front of our house once again on this last Monday before school will end for the summer. As every other weekday the children have been waiting to be picked up, but this morning they are noisier, apparently filled with the excitement of their forthcoming vacation. I wonder what changes this summer will bring... will we be here to see them board that bus again in September?...I find I want to seize every moment of simple ambiance around me while we are still here.....every day life as seen from my cozy office where my days have evolved from weeks to months into years. There is an overwhelming emotion stirring at the very bottom of my soul, that familiar sentiment bringing with it the realization that I am about to close yet another chapter of my life. Each time it seems more difficult to let go but of course I know I must....

August 6, 12:49 am, Sunday morning: I can't sleep there is too much on my mind...not to awaken John I tip-toed quietly out of the room making my way down the dark hallway. It has been a sweltering hot day but finally there is a cool breeze blowing through the open windows. It is a beautiful star lit night and a quarter moon is shining down on us in Lake Elizabeth. It is now very still outside; the next-door neighbors just quit splashing around in their pool. Only porch lights from the homes on the hill in front of the house are illuminating the night. The trees and tall sunflowers are casting ominous black shadows as the wind sways them to and fro creating strange changing images inside on the living room wall where I am now sitting alone in the dark.

I am wondering what the future will bring...should I start packing or will we end up staying here? Good thing I have become more flexible, able to wait to see what the next day will bring... when I was married to Dave plans were always laid out in advance but even then we could not predict what our future held.

I went to get a drink of water from the refrigerator and there in the freezer sat the "Snow Angel" all wrapped in plastic, now only half the size it was when John sculptured it for me after the first snowfall of 1990...ten years ago. During many of those years it was accompanied on the bare shelves only by the loaves of bread Ursula had sent us from the German Bakery. Overwhelmed with emotion, tears well as I recall the excitement, love and passion John and I shared then. Through all our troublesome times we have weathered the storm and with the guidance of that strength maybe the best for us is yet to come?

As my father wrote when he was awaiting trial on charges of war crimes, *"Wasn't it yesterday I shared my joys and sorrows with you?"* And I have, right here in front of the computer I have poured out my heartfelt emotions to you the reader - sharing both joys and sorrows during this special time period during my life as a writer.

I have lived completely consumed by my past these last 12 years of my life. The *inner voice* convinced me at the very beginning of my writing that I needed to take that extraordinary journey into my father's and family's past and later to continue by introducing that *Abandoned Other Child*, finally allowing her to become a renewed part of me.

Consequently I once again find myself at the crossroads, ready to take the next path to yet another whole new unknown exciting episode and close these chapters of my life.

My story is certainly not an uncommon premise, but one that has taken me a lifetime to acknowledge.

"We would never learn to be brave and patient if there were only joy in the world"

......Helen Keller

The End

Epilogue

An uneventful summer had passed and in September 2000 we were still there in Lake Elizabeth and I was still waiting for things to progress on my book. The long yellow school bus once again picked up the children in front of our house, as another Fall semester began.

My nephew Kye had a relapse while vacationing in Europe and continued with more aggressive chemotherapy treatments. He came for a visit on September 1st and I wanted to share this recent manuscript with him. He had already read *The Auschwitz Kommandant,* which created an even closer bond between us. I asked him to write a short summary and here are some of his personal thoughts about this story.

My Thoughts,
September 15, 2000

As I read your story "The Other Child-Abandoned" it was very emotional for me. I suspect I won't be able to give you much insight into the story's appeal to a general audience....I'm too close to it! I found that the story fills in many areas of my own life that were affected by things that happened to you and the family. From my perspective as a child and a young adult I only saw pieces of what affected both of our families. So I found a lot of the gaps were filled in through your story.

I found the piece on my Mom {Brigitte} especially moving because of the time you spent with her and the comfort that it must have brought to her. I wasn't very good at handling the emotions coming from me and her during that illness. I wish I would have been more supportive to her during that time. I hope she knew that I loved her and my way of dealing with it was to maintain some distance. It tore me apart to see her pain and suffering, I now know I could have done more to give her the comfort she needed. Having her sister there, especially at the end, must have been of great support and comfort. She would be very proud to see what you have accomplished with both books. As you know she and others had a difficult time in dealing with the past. For me information and facts are power and I know you have discovered that by knowing the facts and putting them down on paper gives these things a whole new perspective.

I like the story as it is because it's our family's story which has given us all a look at our own past.

No matter what happens with your books I'm impressed at your ability to take this on....and being the one that sees it through. You have had an amazing life so far and I see good things ahead.

With Love,
Kye

On Saturday January 6, 2001 I called Kye, who was now at the City of Hope Hospital lying *under a protective bubble.* He had just completed his last difficult *stem cell* treatment. He seemed to be doing fairly well at this point and ready to go home to get on with his life.

Kye is doing miraculously well. He has returned to work and is in the process of buying a lovely new home.

On January 10, 2001, an unexpected phone call brought my book project - which I believed was just at the verge of receiving a green light, plus everything I had been working toward, to a sudden halt. Wow, how quickly it can all come crashing down along with the dreams and broken promises! I found myself misrepresented and betrayed by the people who had been working with me and as a result I was hurled into a deep dark abyss consumed with fear and anxiety. Had I wasted ten years for nothing? Three long months passed before I emerged from that darkness, but finally I had a whole new team of professionals to guide me, and once again I was focused toward the right direction. But soon even that possibility fell through and once again I had to pick up the shattered pieces. It was at that time I reconnected with my friend Jann who had helped me at the very onset of my writing and once again using her wonderful talent, she was there to pull things together for me.

It's January 2002 and our situation here does not seem to have changed much. It is 10° outside this morning - icicles are hanging off the rooftop and it is very cold in the house. We burned the last of our

*existing firewood last night - a rose trellis from the front yard and a
wooden door stop... something has got to give!*

   ***June 2002**.... After almost five years of living with the unsettling
uncertainty of a pending move - this house we have now lived in for over
7 years has finally been sold. I am busy packing and as of today we
have 30 days to find a new home...I wonder where it will be?*

   *As I sit alone contemplating my predicament surrounded by
stacked boxes, wondering once again what my future may hold at this
point - my thoughts were interrupted by the ringing of the telephone. It
was ZDF Television in Germany whose department of Contemporary
History has invited me and my sister Antje to take part in a documentary
which they are producing about Hitler's SS for the History Channel.
They would also like to do a special short segment on "The Daughters
of the Kommandant" - an insight into how the children of Nazi
perpetrators have been able to cope with the facts of their father's
involvement.*

   *Rather stunned but filled with excitement I wondered if this
could be the vehicle which will finally launch my book project?*

   Things happened quickly and as a result I took a whirlwind four-
day trip to Berlin in July 2002 where I met up with my sister Antje. In
association with ZDF television and their delightful producer Friederike
Dreykluft, we worked on the production in and around the town of
Oranienburg where I was born. Both programs aired in Germany the
following November and seemed to have sparked quite an interest. But no
one would have believed the dire circumstances I had left behind at home
at the time; boxes had been packed up for months without anywhere to go
and I traveled with very little spending money. For a few short days I was
treated like a celebrity for the TV production, but when I returned home I
had to once again face the stark reality of our desperate situation. As the
deadline for the move crept closer we were still uncertain of where to go,
rekindling those familiar fears of being homeless. But before long by a
strange twist of fate, which actually seemed more like a miracle, I had
been hurled even further into the past.

Autumn 2002 *...I just watched the sun come up over the horizon and across the open hills surrounding us - from our new backyard in the Conejo Valley - a hungry coyote was chasing after a small cotton-tailed rabbit. Remarkably my dream of living on a hill has been answered. John and I moved from Lake Elizabeth and somehow find ourselves in Newbury Park perched quite high on top of a ridge in a home which has a breathtaking panoramic view overlooking my old neighborhood of Thousand Oaks. We are able to stay here until this home is razed to make room for a brand new home to be constructed on this site. Once again I am near my family and slowly I seem to be recapturing what had been missing in my life for some time. Chris and Mari are our neighbors, this property belongs to Mari's employer. - Whendy, Drake and Miranda are together again after their separation, living on the Ranch near Santa Barbara and my nephew Kye, Kriste and Nicholas are only five minutes away. It's almost too good to be true, but how odd to be back here reliving so many memories with conflicting emotions. October 20th would have been my 40th wedding anniversary. I don't really understand it, but there must be a reason why I had to return after so many years.*

Today December 30th is so very significant, as I sadly remember another day here fourteen long years ago. Like today, the sun was shining on a beautiful warm afternoon when I kissed my sister Brigitte good-bye for the day, leaving her sleeping quietly at her home at 2850 Calle Damasco. I didn't know it then but it would be our final farewell. Brigitte's home is only a short distance from here and I have since revisited all of the other nearby former family neighborhoods. But without a doubt it is 2850 Calle Damasco which still calls to me from the past - holding a captivating allure - tugging at my heart, searching and longing for a glimpse of the comfort and security which that home once held for me. However, I am of course aware that I cannot bring back those days, but returning here after having left only a few short months after Brigitte's death has helped to bring on the perceivable reality of her passing.

Seems the days are now reminiscent of the beginning when I wrote:

"It is difficult to revisit the past, but I will have to confront those memories and follow that path to see where it will take me..."

This morning through low hanging clouds I watched with a piercing unexplained emptiness in my heart as John headed down our long steep drive in his old Cadillac. It brought back memories of a much happier time long ago when I watched from my apartment balcony as he drove off in his convertible with his blond hair blowing in the wind. An exciting passionate time in our lives when we didn't seem to have many cares, until my dreams were lost to bitter reality. Today when John reached the road below he looked up and waved, gripping me with an intense sadness recalling the years we have shared together. Why did it seem like a final departure as he disappeared into the misty fog?

I am still very in tune with that "inner voice" which clearly came to me so long ago telling me to be patient. Now I understand the reason. Along with this story, the year is quickly approaching its' end. I have overcome many adversities, but it has also been an interesting and eventful year filled with many blessings for which I am immensely grateful. I will always cherish yesterday's memories, but hope to make new ones as I now intend to stop living my life in the past. I wonder?

Our time here in this affluent area, on top of this lovely hillside is temporary. Within a years time this enchanting older home will be replaced with a new estate on this extensive piece of property. Therefore I will take special pleasure in every precious moment as I begin another year accompanied by renewed anticipation and excitement.
At the onset of 2003 I had written this in my journal...

Dear Diary!

You're not going to believe what happened today! It's almost impossible to forget the past when it is all around me.... This afternoon I spotted HIM in a parking lot in Thousand Oaks. It has been fifteen years since I ran into this acquaintance at a neighborhood "Pub" and we later had meetings in the park during those difficult days before Brigitte passed away. Today without any feelings of emotion but filled with complete surprise I watched in amazement as he got out of his car - looking almost the same as he did then - sophisticated -still driving a

*classy car - wearing an elegant silk shirt with designer slacks. However
I also noticed that suave familiar walk was a little more rigid and his
perfectly groomed hair was now gray at the temples. He seemed to be
looking around for something or someone and then disappeared into a
building. Seeing him again made me realize how my life had changed -
how I had changed over those last years. But when I saw the sign above
the building that read "Old English Pub" it seemed obvious his life had
continued its' predictable routine. Was he still searching and whom
might he be meeting today? He never noticed me and I went away that
day with a great sense of relief…..*

My journal continues of our life on the hill:

2/21/03: The saga continues as we have 'till end of April here on Alice
Ann Road. Can't get any answers from John he won't talk about what to
do. So I will have to just think about what I have to do. Which is
something I have not found any solutions to as yet? It is a scary thing to
face at this point in my life but I will make it somehow. I can work! I just
want my own little place with my own things around me, some time to
find myself and do what I want to do. However the cost of living is too
high here in this area and it is still too difficult to be here with the daily
reminders from the past. I will miss Chris and Mari, he has been
wonderful but I also feel I am already a burden to him. I know he does
worry about me, although I've told him I am not his responsibility and I
need to figure things out by myself, at my own pace. I don't think he
understands that I can't live up to his expectations. He doesn't
comprehend the relationship between John and myself. I'm confused too
and don't even know what it is I should do next. I think we both agree we
don't want to live together and I do not want to live with my children!

2/23/03: Called Whendy yesterday about living possibilities in Lompoc
where I know things are more reasonable. She called this morning, saying
that today they are going to Solvang and she will look around and pick up
newspapers on housing and jobs for me. She said I would like quaint
Solvang or Buellton but probably not Lompoc. I feel better already at the
thought of a smaller town and at least closer to Whendy, if not here with
Chris.

Mom Ursula thinks I should come live in her vacant condo, in Las Vegas. It's a nice offer, which I need to think about more seriously.

I have already sent my car key to Jesse Valdez at LV Automotive where my Datsun 280 ZX is parked, to check what kind of repairs my car needs. Chris said he would help with the cost of the repairs so I would have transportation?

When I ask John what he thought was wrong with my car and that I had sent Jesse my key, he became furious. He ended up telling Jesse he will be there to take a look at it himself. He's very possessive of it - says he feels about it like his old Porsche and I'm an Indian giver. I did change my mind when I realized I needed my car, because it was at least paid for and John was not doing anything with it anyway. After my divorce, it was the first car I had ever bought and paid for on my own. Not helping me to get my car running all these years was surely a controlling factor by John to keep me at home. I had always suspected it, but wasn't ready to make any waves.

3/3/03: Last week John and I argued for three days when I was trying to get some answers from him on what he thought we might do next. No conclusions but we have made a truce "till end of March" when we should know when we must leave here. As always after stressful days, I developed a terrible headache.

Today is another laundry day. I walked next door to Chris and Mari's mud room where I do the wash every Monday when they're gone.

It's cloudy with the wonderful fragrance of approaching rain in the air. From the other side of the double doors which lead into the mud room I am always greeted with a fresh clean scent. Through the windows inside the room, which adjoins their dining and kitchen area, there is a spectacular view of the surrounding green hillsides and large estate size homes. Down below where the street meets our road, a horse is grazing in the pasture. There is a haunting sadness tugging at my heart because soon it will all be over.

Oh how I'll miss these special Mondays on our hill - here where I am once again close to my son. The washer is now shaking the soft termite infested old wooden floor of their house, which is however not evident on the surface, because Mari keeps the floors and the entire house spotless.

With the laundry done I always leave, what Mari calls *a little treasure.* At Christmas time it was one of Chris' childhood Advent Calendars from the early 1970's. Today it will be a tiny pewter angel; sometimes it's only a note to say *I Love You.*

3/5/03: Last night Kye and Kriste brought another battery and power pack for the small lap top computer which they gave me years ago.

Our own problems at the moment seem so insignificant because they are talking of going to war with Iraq in two weeks. Why can't they settle it some other way! All those young men and women from ages 21 deployed for that region, it breaks my heart.

I wonder how this will effect the possibility to sell my book? God I wish I would get some good news on it soon. I don't think Whendy or even Chris believe that it will ever happen. I feel like Chris has given up on me, but then he has so much going on in his own life. I hope and pray that all of his efforts and endeavors will materialize for him and that his screen play will sell.

3/29/03: Have been looking into job possibilities here, filled out applications and had several calls. Also looked into apartment availability's but don't know how I'd be able to make it here on my own. The most reasonable one bedroom rents for $850 a month but John is not interested in living in a small apartment with me?

I even inquired at the old apartment complex where I first lived as a newlywed with my husband, over 40 years ago. My God what emotions that brought forth. It's even lovelier now with tall trees and lush landscaping, back then they had been newly constructed apartments. I can't see me living here among all these memories from the past!

4/28/03: Contacted my friend Ellie with whom I used to work at *Lim's Fashions* in Westlake. Inquired about job possibilities at the Library where she works. Told her about my dilemma and she thought Las Vegas would be a good move. It was so nice to talk to her and she was full of compassion and concern when she realized the distressing state I was in. I was in need of a friend but everything seems so devastating.

6/13/03: John and I took another drive through the beautiful Lake Sherwood area. He stopped to take pictures of a large estate size home on the lake which he would like to own. The photos will help him to visualize, he believes this will draw it closer into reality for him. I understand the concept behind his theories but I don't need a mansion, I just wish I had a home to call my own. Such big dreams and nothing to support the manifestation into actuality!

7/21/03: Today the historic *Edelweiss Restaurant* in Palmdale went up in flames. It had formerly been owned and operated by our friends Renate Witte and Wulf Loenicker. It was also at this enchanting landmark where I first met John, a poignant tangible reminder of what turned out to be the turning point, which drastically changed my life, almost fourteen years ago. Ironically this fire was a very obvious physical sign which indicated to me that like the loss of the *Edelweiss,* this chapter of my life was rapidly coming to an end. It will always have a very special meaning to John and me, and as we watched the news on TV with picture footage of the restaurant completely engulfed in flames, we just hugged each other tearfully.

7/24/03: Today Proflame came for the last time to fill our propane tank with $25.00 worth of gas. It should last about 3 to 4 weeks and if we run out it will be cold showers again or maybe we'll hook up the Bar-B-Q tank until we leave here.

8/5/03 Tues. Another beautiful sunset here on the hill. John is soaking in the tub, while I'm alone out here watching the spectacular sky turn from bright orange to soft hues of pink. Shades of light and charcoal gray clouds look like painted streaks of watercolors across the horizon. The images are changing rapidly and the colors are becoming more brilliant against the background of dark silhouettes and shadows of purple mountains in the distance. This is such an incredible experience - I think of you Brigitte my dear sister. For more than 25 years you used to work just over the hill across the freeway. I feel you here with me tonight and find myself sobbing. Why can't you be here with me now? I've come home to you - but I'm homeless. In three weeks we have to leave here. I wish I knew the answers as what to do next? Should I stay or start over in some foreign, strange place like Las Vegas?

I'm observing a cotton-tail bunny nibbling on the few remaining patches of green grass. His large ears perked up, he stopped and looked at me as I entered the sun room where John has his exercise equipment. I sat down on the bench, while undisturbed by my presence; he continues to keep his curious watchful eye on me. We really have become so very close to nature here. How I will miss it all - the rabbits, ground squirrels, hawks, owls, our roadrunner, the coyotes who come for our leftovers. What will happen to them when the construction crew plows up the unspoiled land? It's been a piece of heaven, although our time here has been filled with despair.

8/11/03 Out in the sun room once more, only it's nighttime, actually 1:45 am. I have another excruciating headache, the pain is unbearable but only one of the reasons I can't sleep. This time it is so debilitating that I have been in bed for 3 days, that's never happened before and I can't keep anything down. Down below the town is barely awake but lights are still twinkling and traffic lights are changing from vivid red to green, while above the full moon is drawing what energies I have left at this point.

I still don't know what John is going to do at the end of the month. When I ask, he says *"I don't owe you any explanation about what I'm going to do and you don't owe me any."* I told him *"But after all the time we've been together I do at least feel I owe you the courtesy of letting you know what I am planning!"* Does he really not care or is he so hurt and afraid that his only defense is to lash out at me? I'm so confused and disillusioned because I really do care about what happens to him but I also resent his attitude and lack of consideration. Why can't we do something and put some effort into helping each other? He asked me *"What have YOU done all these years?"* I reminded him, *"I have written three books that's including the work on Renate's".* Has he forgotten how adamant he was, about me not going to work but stressing that I should concentrate on my writing? At least I am willing to do anything I have to at this point, but it now looks like I am on my own.

I'm packing and getting rid of things while he is working out and watching his TV ministers [at a deafening volume, which is not helping my nerves]. He hasn't been playing his favorite ***"Elvis, Buddy Holly, Bo Diddley rock'n roll "50's"*** music lately because he knows the noise has bothered my headaches. Guess he needs a place of his own where he can play his music whenever he wants, as loud as he pleases.

I only hope he will be moved out by the 31st.

I don't even get straight answers about my car, still a game for him to control, right to the last minute. Or maybe he just "liberated" it, as he has a habit of doing with things he really wants for himself? But right now I don't have the finances to register and insure it anyway, never mind the gasoline to fill it, or the fact it is not running right. So I don't know how to get me and my stuff to Las Vegas. Yesterday Kye came to see me after I talked to Kriste, his wife. He was concerned about me and thought a move to Vegas would be a good decision right now, also said they could take me to Vegas if I needed a ride. How wonderful that he wants to help me.

Somehow I'm functioning but in a numb and listless state of disbelief. I feel so alone, how could it have come to this and what happened to my partner? If he really loved me wouldn't he have been motivated to do something - anything? My suggestion for both of us to take a job and look for a small apartment was met with obvious resentment. Since he does not want to live in a tiny apartment, I asked him if he'd rather live in his van. He didn't think that was too bad. I also let him know I would never do that again, once was enough for me! He is not trying to stop me from leaving and has not asked me to stay, probably realizing we cannot live together under these circumstances.

Anyway, I've decided to make things easier on myself. The Salvation Army will pick up all of my furniture; only the china cabinet is sold. It will be heartbreaking to let go of the beautiful wall unit, which used to belong to my sister Brigitte and the walnut dining table, which goes back 40 years. Every family member had sat around it throughout the years, enjoying the warmth of those special dinners. It was a part of my children's growing-up years and I recall how they used to hide their vitamins down within the cracks of the base. It was also difficult getting rid of the Bar-B-Q that Kye had given us three years ago when he was so ill. It was often the only cook stove we had. I cleaned it and gave it to a very deserving lady whose husband had left her and her children. She hugged me and we both had tears but of course for different reasons.

Only the boxes and few remaining things will go into storage. And finally I signed my car over to John. This is all too surreal and extremely difficult but I feel somewhat of a relief after I made those important decisions. I always remember my former husband used to tell me what he had learned in the army, which was to make the best decision you could, and then act on it, whether you were sure if it was right or wrong at the time.

8/15/03: Today John and I shared a very special moment in history together. We watched with great excitement and emotion, waving from the top of our hill as the *Air Force One* helicopter, along with a group of others' in formation, flew over and landed only half a mile away from our house. Quickly President Bush was swept off into a motorcade to make a speech in Thousand Oaks about National Park conservation.

8/20/03: Today is John's birthday and I can't allow my sadness to interfere with the celebration. My gift to him was a new pair of his favorite shoes, which I always bought for him at Penneys. My card to him said *"Hope these will take you places you've never been!"* [a phrase he once used on me a long time ago when we first met] *"I will always be here for you if you need me and I will always love You"*.

Chris and Mari took us to the nice mesquite BBQ restaurant on the hill in Simi Valley. We all knew it was our last birthday with John, but we all tried to cover up what we were really feeling. It was a wonderful dinner but as we left, John said, *"That felt like the Last Supper!"*

We walked out together holding hands, the way we used to years ago when we were dating, and I wished that the moment would never end.

Later Chris and Mari came over to our house bringing pie and ice cream for dessert. This and watching movies had become a familiar ritual between us four on the hill. We sat together in the empty, spacious front room for the last time, surrounded only by stacked boxes. Today there were no heavenly angel figures smiling down at us from my cherished wall unit, which was already taken away by the Salvation Army. No more candles burning to enhance a tranquil atmosphere.

Chris gave John a gift of two books, the third volume of *Conversations with God* - John had given Chris the first book years ago - and a new *Dream Encyclopedia,* along with an extraordinary card which so profoundly read:

"It's all about the Journey" .

Reading through last years' journal this particular passage catches my eye....

"Early this morning, sitting alone in the dark, all the main characters found throughout these written pages are here with me within my thoughts to replay the drama. From that exciting crossing of the Atlantic with my new parents at age 13 as I left behind "the child"...where would I have ended up had they not adopted me?....to those coming of age years in New York which are difficult to recall.... my summer as a California girl.... my life as a wife and mother.... and most important the time my sister Brigitte came back into my life giving me a sense of belonging, knowing that I had roots....real parents and siblings who truly loved me long before the time of my adoption, filling in that lonely gap....and then the past decade of self discovery finally realizing I no longer had to live my life in secrecy and shame, a time which strangely enough led me back full circle to the very beginning to face those facts I believed had to be hidden. There is now a healing closure to all those years where deep within me was a longing and need for "The Abandoned Other Child"

...... but suddenly the tranquil stillness of night is shattered, that magic spell brought on by my vivid imaginary visions is interrupted with the

haunting cries of coyotes - their howling is carried on the wind from the distant hills - somewhere across the moonlit lake...."

So unlike myself, John was not ready to look for work and find a place to live. He was heading toward a whole new direction, which he claimed "was a calling". He made his decision and chose the life of a lone transient, simply letting destiny guide him. He seemed to have no second thoughts about leaving and as sad as that was I was also relieved to turn my life around and that of course, had to be without John.

Two weeks later John and I embraced before I left the hillside in Newbury Park for the last time so ending the fourteen years I had shared with him. This time it was John who waved to me from the top of the hill until I reached the end of the road below. Confused and distressed – with great emotion I looked up and watched him disappear from sight as I anxiously headed down the highway toward Las Vegas and an uncertain future.

Update 2003 – 2009

Once again my mom was there to rescue me and I went to live in Ursula's condo on Sloan Lane in Las Vegas. It was to be another temporary stopover until I could find some new direction for my life. It was comfortable and vacant as she was living with her companion Charlie, giving me time alone to get over my break-up after the fourteen- year relationship with John.

The first day alone at the condo brought back a flood of memories as I looked around her charming little residence. It was more like I had returned to a place which was once considered home.   I discovered some familiar items taking me back to my childhood after Ursula and Earl adopted me, such as the old fashioned pin cushion, Ursula's small ivory bowling trophy inscribed **_Nuremberg Women's League 1955-56;_** it had turned to a shade of brown. There was the wooden paddle inscribed: **_Bottom Whopper – Seneca Knolls, NY_**, where we had lived. In the kitchen I noticed the large **_"Homer Laughlin"_** ceramic bowl with the trim of blue stripes and gold painted leaves. Mom used it for her potato salad back in Fayetteville, NY, after we came to America.

I looked through the many photo albums and every room was filled with a montage of family photographs covering the walls, an array of old and new. Their images held haunting recollections like the old beautiful oil paintings and then there was the watercolor of an adorable Dale at age 2, in 1954. There used to be a likeness of me as well, but it was nowhere in sight and within the old frame was a new family portrait of Ursula, Dale and sister Gale. I think it was discarded a long time ago, during those years Ursula and I were estranged from one another.

But to my surprise there on a shelf was the model of a black stretch limousine which John had sent to Ursula years ago. Inscribed on the top was "Ursula's Dream Machine". He had promised her that he would pick her up in such a limousine when he became a success, but that one would have to do until that time came.

John later wrote to me in Las Vegas and sent a picture.
In my Journal I noted:

"I could hardly focus through the tears, looking at the photograph of him, it tugged at my heartstrings. His familiar face yet a complete stranger was looking back at me – gaunt with long hair – sitting in front of the tent which he and his cat Rosebud now call home. Only a month ago we were living on top of "the hill", still sharing the same home. I wonder how he really feels about living the life of a transient hippie? My God this is all too surreal!

The following January 2004 I went to live with my daughter Whendy, Drake and Miranda at the ranch in Santa Barbara. I stayed for a three months trial period, but decided then that the Santa Barbara area was not for me. However, I found my daughter also needed me at that time and looking back now I am so grateful for those three months we had together.

I returned to Las Vegas where I had met Charlie's son and we soon began to date, becoming better acquainted. By October 2004 I moved to his eight acres in the remote community of Boulevard, California, near the Mexican border.

Before I left Las Vegas for the last time I wrote in my Journal:

Dear Diary,

Today my fourteen year relationship with John came to its' final conclusion. With haunting reminiscence of the life we once shared together, I slowly removed his Star Ruby ring from my finger for the last time. The intricately shaped white gold band is set with one tiny diamond next to a bright pink oval stone, from which center bursts a brilliant sparkling six pointed star.

I recall the day so long ago, when he had found it in a second hand store in Palmdale. His face lit up with that illuminating smile and as he placed it on my finger he told me, "I have been looking for one to match my own for some time…now we are Soul-Mates Forever!"

The definition of "Forever" is: eternal continuance without beginning or end"…. Are our experiences here on this physical plane only a small fragment of an endless Journey?….

Life became easier in Boulevard with my new companion, at least for a time, and continues quietly and tranquil as I still work on getting The Auschwitz Kommandant published. I was also inspired to do more writing surrounded by my natural environment shared by coyotes, huge rabbits, shiny black ravens, quail, our roadrunner and sometimes even deer.

However 2006 would be the year of my most difficult personal trial yet. The challenging circumstances involving the tragic destiny of my daughter Whendy and my nephew Kye, have me facing a future I certainly never expected. Somehow I am coping a day at a time by once again writing about these experiences. But this time it is different, the lingering pain is unrelenting as I attempt to heal my broken heart within the pages of what is the title of my next book:

"When the Morning-glories Bloom I'll Think of You "
"A Mother's Loving Tribute to her Daughter"

In 2009 History Press in the UK published *The Auschwitz Kommandant– A Daughter's Search for the Father She Never Knew.*

It had not been an easy road, but my relentless determination to never give up continuously recalled those words I heard so long ago *"You will succeed".*

Made in the USA
Middletown, DE
10 November 2016